cute knit hats
for kids

cute knit hats for kids

36 projects

Jenny Occleshaw

STACKPOLE BOOKS

Dedication

I would like to dedicate this book to my beautiful daughter Felicity, who has survived all manner of peculiar knitted and crocheted creations throughout her life and has lived to tell the tale, and to Fin and Elsie, who are an endless source of inspiration and joy in my life.

First published in 2012 by New Holland Publishers (UK) Ltd
London • Cape Town • Sydney • Auckland
www.newhollandpublishers.com

Garfield House	Wembley Square	Unit 1, 66 Gibbes Street	218 Lake Road
86–88 Edgware Road	First Floor, Solan	Chatswood	Northcote
London W2 2EA, UK	Road Gardens	New South Wales 2067	Auckland
	Cape Town 8001	Australia	New Zealand
	South Africa		

Published in the United States of America in 2013 by Stackpole Books, 5067 Ritter Rd., Mechanicsburg, PA 17055
www.stackpolebooks.com

10 9 8 7 6 5 4 3 2 1

ISBN 978-0-8117-1254-5
A catalogue record of this book is available at the National Library of Australia and The British Library

Publishing Manager: Lliane Clarke
Senior Editor: Simona Hill
Photographer: Graham Gillies
Illustrator: Steve Dew
Designer: Kimberley Pearce
Production Director: Olga Dementiev
Cover Design: Wendy Reynolds

Printed and bound Toppan Leefung (China) Ltd

Author's Note

Please enjoy making these patterns. They are not for commercial reproduction. For assistance with patterns contact Drop Stitch Designs (jennyoccleshaw@hotmail.com).

Publisher's Note

Some of the hats are made with small parts that may be a choking hazard to a young child or baby. Make sure such elements are sewed firmly in place and check them regularly. If in doubt, do not add them to the hats.

Contents

Introduction

The hats and beanies in this book are all made with either DK-weight yarn or baby yarn. While I have generally not specified a particular brand I recommend that you use pure wool for these knits since it is resilient and also available in a broad range of lovely colors. Pure wool is warm and cosy to wear and is much kinder on knitters' hands. When selecting yarns, use the weight specified; otherwise your hat may end up the wrong size.

These beanies are mostly knitted in the round, meaning that you will either work with three double-pointed needles, with the number of stitches split equally between the three needles, or you will use a circular needle. Circular needles are made in different lengths. Generally, a loop of thick plastic holds the needles together. Look for circular needles that are 16 in. long; with shorter needles, you will have to stretch the yarn too much in order to join the ends into a circle.

When working with multiple yarns, make sure you carry the colors not in use behind the knitted work. Be careful not to pull the yarn too tightly or this will create a puckered effect. When joining a new color, twist the two colors together at the back of the work so that you don't create a hole, and always leave a long tail of yarn at the start and end of any color addition so that you have ends to weave in.

Sew all decorative features on very securely. This cannot be overstated. Some of the hats have very small parts such as beads and buttons, which can be a hazard for even the youngest baby. If in doubt, omit these details and embroider them instead with stranded cotton embroidery floss.

I recommend that you gather all your supplies together before you begin a project and take your time when knitting. Start with a simple project from the beginning of the book if you are a novice knitter and progress to more complex items as you gain confidence. Recipients of your hats will be absolutely thrilled, so it's worth taking the time to get the designs just right.

Abbreviations

Beg: beginning
Cont: continue
Dec: decrease
In.: inches
Inc: increase the number of stitches indicated
K: knit
K2tog: knit next 2 stitches together
M1: make 1 stitch by picking up the loop that lies between the two needles and knitting into the back
P: purl
P2tog: purl next 2 stitches together
Psso: pass slipped stitch over
P2sso: pass 2 slipped stitches over
Rep: repeat
Sl: slip
Ssk: slip, slip knit next 2 stitches together
St: stitch
Sts: stitches
St st: stockinette stitch
Rem: remaining
Rep: repeat
RS: right side
Tbl: through back of loops
Tog: together
WS: wrong side
Yo: yarn over

Crochet Abbreviations

Ch: chain
Dc: double crochet
Dt: double treble crochet
Hd: half double crochet
Sc: single stitch
Sl st: slip stitch
Tr: treble crochet

Busy Bee

This is a hat for a little baby, knitted in very soft baby wool. It's a simple ribbed knit with plenty of stretch for maximum comfort. Feelers and embroidered bees turn it into something very special. The embroidered bees are created using rows of bullion knots.

Size
To fit 6–9 months

Materials

1 x 50 g ball black baby yarn
1 x 50 g ball pale yellow baby yarn
Stranded cotton embroidery floss
  in white, black, and yellow

Size 3 (3.25 mm) knitting needles
Yarn needle
Embroidery needle
Chenille pipe cleaners (optional)

Hat

Using size 3 knitting needles, and black yarn, cast on 115 sts.
Work in k1, p1 ribbing and stripe pattern as follows until work measures 5 1/2 in. from cast-on edge.

Stripe Pattern

4 rows rib: black
4 rows rib: pale yellow

Crown Shaping

Continuing the stripe pattern, work:
Dec row 1: K1, p1, (k3tog, p1, k1, p1) 18 times, k3tog, p1, k1 (77 sts).
Work 3 rows in ribbing without shaping.
Dec row 2: K1, (p3tog, k1) 19 times (39 sts).
Work 1 row in ribbing without shaping.
Dec row 3: K1, (p2tog, k2tog) to end (20 sts).
Break off yarn. Thread through rem sts, pull up tightly, and fasten off.
Sew seam, reversing seam at lower third to allow for turning brim.

Feelers

Using size 3 knitting needles and black yarn, cast on 7 sts.
Beg with a knit row, work in st st for 2 3/4 in. Cast off.

Finishing Roll up lengthwise. Insert a chenille pipe cleaner into each feeler and sew closed. This is not strictly necessary, but does make the bee's feelers stand straight. Attach the feelers to the top of the hat, spacing them evenly. Make sure that the stitching is firm.

Embroidered Bees

There are 9 embroidered bees on the hat, 4 on the brim and 5 on the body of the hat. Use pins to mark the positions for your bees so that you are happy with the placement.

Using 3 strands of black embroidery floss, make a 6-wrap bullion knot for the tail. Leave a little space.
Make a 9-wrap bullion knot parallel to the first, leaving the width of one bullion knot between the stitches. Leave a little space.
Next, make a 7-wrap bullion knot. Leave a little space.
Make a 5-wrap bullion knot for the head.
Work 2 straight stitches as feelers protruding at angles from the top of the head.
Using 3 strands of yellow embroidery floss and, starting at the tail end of the bee, make an 8-wrap bullion knot in the space between the 6- and 9-wrap bullion knots.

Make an 11-wrap bullion knot in the space between the 9- and 7-wrap bullion knots.

Make an 8-wrap bullion knot in the space between the 7- and 5-wrap bullion knots.

Wings

Using 3 strands of white embroidery floss, bring the needle out at the 11-wrap yellow bullion knot. Make 2 lazy daisy stitches on each side of the bee's body for wings.

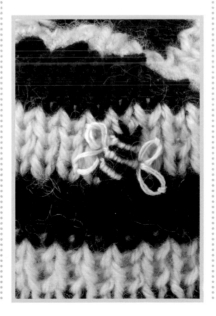

Apple Blossom

This is a delightful hat for any little girl who loves pink. The ruffles are crocheted onto the hat base once the hat is knitted. Little beaded flowers are stitched onto the crown, though they can be left off if you think they are likely to be chewed or pulled off.

Sizes

To fit 18 months to 2 years (instructions for 3 to 4 years in parentheses)

Materials

1 x 50 g ball bright pink DK yarn
1 x 50 g ball pale pink DK yarn
1 x 50 g ball cream DK yarn
Small amounts of bright pink and cream baby yarn for the flowers
6 (7) crystal beads for the flower centers

Size 6 (4 mm) double-pointed knitting needles
Yarn needle
Size D-3 (3.25 mm) crochet hook
White sewing thread
Beading needle

Hat

Using the size 6 double-pointed knitting needles and bright pink, cast on 90 (100) sts. Join to work in round, being careful not to twist the stitches. Thread a loop of a different color yarn onto the needle to indicate the start/end of a row.

Rounds 1–10: Knit.
Break off the bright pink and join the pale pink.
Rounds 11: Knit.
Join the cream yarn.
Rounds 12–23: *K1 with pale pink, p1 with cream; rep from * to end. Carry along the unused yarn neatly behind each stitch.
Break off pale pink and continue in cream.
Round 24: Purl.
Rounds 25–34: Knit.

Round 35: Purl.
Rounds 36–43: Knit.
Round 44: Purl.
Rounds 45–50: Knit.
Round 51: Purl.
Rounds 52–54: Knit.
Round 55: Purl.

Crown Shaping

Join pale pink.
Round 56: With pale pink, *K7 (8), k2tog; rep from * to end of round.
Round 57: With cream, knit.
Continue to alternate between 1 round of pale pink and 1 round of cream for the rest of the crown.
Round 58: *K6 (7), k2tog; rep from * to end of round.
Round 59: Knit.
Round 60: *K5 (6), k2tog; rep from * to end of round.
Round 61: *K4 (5), k2tog; rep from * to end of round.
Round 62: Knit.
Round 63: *K3 (4), k2tog; rep from * to end of round.
Round 64: Knit.
Round 65: *K2 (3), k2tog; rep from * to end of round.
Round 66: Knit.
Continue decreasing in this pattern until 10 sts remain.
Break off yarn, thread through rem sts, pull up tightly, and fasten off.
Weave in all the ends on the wrong side.

Ruffles

The ruffles are crocheted in rounds of pale pink and bright pink. They are worked into the purl rows knitted into the body of the hat. Work from the brim up.
With a size D crochet hook and pale pink, insert the hook into the first purl loop of the purl row at the top of the rib.
* Ch 3, sc into next purl loop; rep from * all the way around the hat, finishing with a sl st in the first st. Work the other 4 rounds of crochet ruffle the same way.

Flowers

Make 6 for the smaller size and 7 for the larger size, using cream for round 1 and deep pink for round 2.

Using a size D crochet hook, ch 4; join into a ring with a sl st.

Round 1: (right side) Ch 2, work 9 sc in ring, sl st in top of ch-2 (10 sts).

Round 2: Ch 5, work 1 dc in each of next 9 sc, sl st in top of ch-5. Fasten off.

Weave in ends and form into a neat circle.

Using a beading needle threaded with white thread, very firmly sew 1 crystal bead to the center of each flower.

Finishing

Sew one flower to the center of the crown and distribute the other flowers evenly around the crown. Sew firmly in place.

Little Ladybug

This is a simple hat is ideal for less experienced knitters and is perfect for babies to wear. The ladybug's spots are bobbles, which are made separately and attached once the beanie is complete.

Size
To fit 6–9 months

Materials
1 x 50 g ball red baby yarn
Small amount of black baby yarn
Size 3 (3.25 mm) knitting needles
Size 0 (2 mm) knitting needles
Yarn needle

Hat

Using size 3 knitting needles, and red, cast on 115 sts.
Work in k1, p1 rib until work measures 5 1/2 in. from beg.

Shape Top

Dec row 1: K1, p1, (k3tog, p1, k1, p1) 18 times, k3tog, p1, k1 (77 sts). Work 3 rows in ribbing without shaping.
Dec row 2: K1, (p3tog, k1) 19 times (39 sts). Work 1 row in ribbing without shaping.
Dec row 3: K1, (p2tog, k2tog) to end (20 sts).
Break off yarn. Thread through rem sts, pull up tightly, and fasten off. Sew seam, reversing seam at lower third to allow for turning up brim.

Bobbles

Using size 0 knitting needles and black, cast on 1 st.
Row 1: K1, p1, k1, p1, k1 all into same st (5 sts).
Row 2: Purl
Row 3: Knit.
Row 4: Purl
Row 5: Knit all sts. *Sl the second st on right-hand needle over the first; repeat from * until 1 st remains. Fasten off.
Make 12.

Run a gathering thread around the edge of each bobble and draw up to form a round bobble. Weave in one end of the thread and use the other to attach the bobble to the beanie.

Finishing

Attach one bobble to the top of the crown and sew the others randomly around the hat. Turn up the brim.

Baby Flowers

This is a simple hat for a young baby. It's knitted from very soft 4-ply baby yarn and is a good choice for a novice to knit. The gorgeous felt flowers brighten the design. You can use just one color or have a whole array of beautiful blooms. Felted flowers are available from craft shops or online from speciality felt suppliers.

Size
To fit 6–9 months

Materials
1 x 50 g ball cream baby yarn
Size 3 (3.25 mm) knitting needles
Yarn needle
10 felt flowers, 1 ½ in. in diameter
Sewing thread and needle

Hat

Using size 3 knitting needles and cream, cast on 115 sts.
Work in k1, p1 rib until work measures 5 ½ in. from cast-on row.

Crown Shaping

Dec row 1: K1, p1, (k3tog, p1, k1, p1) 18 times, k3tog, p1, k1 (77 sts).
Work 3 rows in ribbing without shaping.
Dec row 2: K1, (p3tog, k1) 19 times (39 sts).
Work 1 row in ribbing without shaping.
Dec row 3: K1, (p2tog, k2tog) to end (20 sts).
Break off yarn. Thread through rem sts, pull up tightly, and fasten off.

Finishing

Sew the seam, reversing the seam on the lower third to allow for turning up the brim.
Turn up a brim of 1 ½ in. Arrange the felt flowers around the hat as desired and pin in place. Sew into position and tie off. Each flower needs to be sewn on individually, rather than carrying the sewing thread around on the inside of the hat, or the hat will lose its stretch. Try not to go through too many knitted stitches when sewing on the flowers.

Cheeky Elf

Most of my inspiration for knitting projects comes from my small grandchildren. There is nothing more satisfying than knitting for those you love. Their adorable elfin faces will look just lovely framed by this elfin hat. Noro variegated yarn provides the striping and little knitted leaves add extra detail. The hat is knitted in the round and finished with a quirky knot.

Sizes

To fit 12 months (instructions for 2 to 3 years given in parentheses)

Materials

1 x 100 g ball self-striping sock yarn
Size 3 (3.25 mm) double-pointed knitting needles
Size 1 (2.25 mm) double-pointed knitting needles
Yarn needle

Hat

Using size 3 double-pointed needles and sock yarn, cast on 92 (112) sts. Join to work in round, being careful not to twist the stitches.

Work 10 rounds st st (knit every round) for rolled brim.

Next work 10 rounds k1, p1 rib.

Continue to work in st st until work measures 5 (5½) in.

Crown Shaping

Dec round 1: *K21 (26), k2tog; rep from * to end of row (88 [108] sts).

Next round and every alternate round: Knit.

Dec round 2: *K20 (25), k2tog; rep from * to end of row (84 [104] sts).

Cont decreasing in this pattern until 12 sts rem. Work on these 12 sts for 2 in.

Next round: (K1, k2tog) 4 times (8 sts).

Cont on these 8 sts until the thinnest part measures 6 in.

Next round: K2tog all round. Break off yarn. Thread through rem sts, pull up tightly, and fasten off.

Finishing

Weave in any loose ends and press lightly if needed. Knot the top knot.

I-Cord Leaves

With size 3 double-pointed needles, cast on 3 sts. Work an I-cord as follows: *Knit all sts. *Do not turn.* Switch right-hand needle to left hand and pull sts to other end of needle. Pull yarn firmly around behind work, ready to knit into the first st again. Repeat from * until I-cord stem measures 1 in.

Now work forward and backward in rows, beginning the first row by switching the work to the left hand without turning and pulling the yarn around behind the work, as in the basic I-cord.

Row 1: Knit.

Row 2: Purl.

Row 3: K1, m1, k1, m1, k1 (5 sts).

Row 4 and all even rows: K1, purl to last st, k1.

Row 5: K2, m1, k1, m1, k2 (7 sts).

Row 7: K3, m1, k1, m1, k3 (9 sts).

Row 9: K4, m1, k1, m1, k4 (11 sts).

Row 11: K5, m1, k1, m1, k5 (13 sts).

Row 13: K5, sl2, k1, p2sso (11 sts).

Row 15: K4, sl2, k1, p2sso (9 sts).

Row 17: K3, sl2, k1, p2sso (7 sts).

Row 19: K2, sl2, k1, p2sso (5 sts).

Row 21: K1, sl2, k1, p2sso (3 sts).

Row 22: Sl1, p2tog, psso (1 st). Fasten off.

Finishing

Press lightly if needed. Weave in ends.

Sew on the leaves at random around the hat.

The Great Gatsby

This beret, scarf, and shoes set reminds me of the tweed caps worn in the 1920s. I wanted to make some patterns that were specifically for boys and I think this is most definitely one of them. The little Fair Isle band and the loops on the crown give the design a more contemporary feel. This is a fairly simple knit.

Size
To fit 6–9 months

Materials

3 x 50 g balls tweedy brown DK yarn

Small amounts of DK yarn in cream, olive green, and fawn

Size 5 (3.75 mm) knitting needles

Size 2 (3 mm) knitting needles

Stitch holder

Size 2 (3 mm) double-pointed knitting needles

Yarn needle

Hat

Using size 5 needles and tweedy brown, cast on 75 sts.

Work in k1, p1 rib for 7 rows.

Inc row 1: P4, (m1, p1, m1, p10) 6 times, m1, p1, m1, p3, m1, p1 (90 sts).

Work Fair Isle pattern over next 7 rows:

Fair Isle Pattern

(10 st repeat, worked over 7 rows)

C: Cream
F: Fawn
G: Olive green

Row 1: K1C, k1G, k4C, k1F k3C
Row 2: P2C, p3F, p2C, p3G.
Row 3: K1G, k1C, k2G, k2C, k1F, k2C, k1G.
Row 4: P2G, p3C, p2G, p3C.
Row 5: K1C, k1F, k2C, k2G, k1C, k2G, k1C.

Row 6: P2C, p3G, p2C, p3F.
Row 7: K1C, k1F, k4C, k1G, k3C.

Continuing in tweedy brown, purl one row, decreasing 1 st (89 sts).

Inc row 2: K5, (m1, k1, m1, k12) 6 times, m1, k1, m1, k5 (103 sts).

Work 5 rows st st.

Inc row 3: K6, (m1, k1, m1, k14) 6 times, m1, k1, m1, k6 (117 sts).

Work 5 rows st st.

Continue in this pattern, increasing 14 sts on the next row and on every following sixth row until there are 159 sts.

Work another 5 rows st st.

Dec row 1: K8, (k2tog, k1, k2tog, k18) 6 times, k2tog, k1, k2tog, k8 (145 sts).

Work 5 rows st st.

Dec row 2: K7, (k2tog, k1, k2tog, k16) 6 times, k2tog, k1, k2tog, k7 (131 sts).

Work 5 rows st st.

Dec row 3: K6, (k2tog, k1, k2tog, k14) 6 times, k2tog, k1, k2tog, k6 (117 sts).

Work 5 rows st st.

Continue in this pattern, decreasing 14 sts on every sixth row until 33 sts remain.

Next row: Purl.
Next row: (K1, k2tog) to end.
Next row: Purl.
Next row: (K1, k2tog) to end.

Break off yarn, thread through rem sts, pull up tightly, and fasten off.

Finishing

Block, if needed. Sew in all ends and, using backstitch or mattress stitch, sew seam.

I-Cord Loops

Using size 2 double-pointed knitting needles, cast on 3 sts. Make an I-cord as follows: *Knit all sts. *Do not turn.* Switch right-hand needle to left hand and pull sts to other end of needle. Pull yarn firmly around behind work, ready to knit into the first st again. Repeat from * until I-cord measures 4 in. Sl1, k2tog, psso. Break off yarn and draw through rem st. Fasten off neatly.

Make 3 I-cords 4 in. long, 1 cream, 1 olive green, and 1 fawn.

Attach loops firmly to top of crown. Loops can be made in different sizes, if you like.

Shoes
Sole

Using size 2 knitting needles and tweedy brown, cast on 3 sts.

Row 1: Knit.

Row 2: Kfb, k1, kfb (5 sts).
Row 3: Kfb, k3, kfb (7 sts).
Row 4: Knit
Row 5: Kfb, k5, kfb (9 sts).
Row 6: Kfb, k7, kfb (11 sts).
Row 7: Knit.
Row 8: Kfb, k9, kfb (13 sts).
Work another 28 rows in garter stitch without shaping.
Dec row 1: K2tog, knit to last 2 sts, k2tog.
Next row: Knit.
Repeat these two rows until 5 sts remain.

Upper
Row 1: Kfb in first 2 sts, k1, kfb in rem 2 sts (9 sts).
Row 2 and all even rows: Purl.
Row 3: [K1, kfb in next 2 sts, k1] twice, k1 (13 sts).
Row 5: [K2, kfb in next 2 sts, k2] twice, k1 (17 sts).

Row 7: K3, kfb, k8, kfb, k4 (19 sts).
Row 10: [P2, kfb] twice, p6, [kfb, p2] twice, p1 (23 sts).
Work another 14 rows in stockinette stitch without shaping.
Row 25: K10, slip these sts to a stitch holder or piece of scrap yarn. Bind off next 3 sts; k10 (10 sts rem on needle).
Row 26 (first side) and every alternate row: Purl.
Row 27: K1, k2tog, k7.
Row 29: K1, k2tog, k6.
Row 31: K1, k2tog, k5.
Work another 15 rows without shaping. Bind off.
Take up sts from stitch holder; rejoin yarn at end of row.
Row 26 (second side) and every alternate row: Purl.
Row 27: K7, ssk, k1.
Row 29: K6, ssk, k1.
Row 31: K5, ssk, k1.

Work another 15 rows without shaping. Bind off.

Edging
With right side facing, using size 2 knitting needles and olive green, pick up and knit 35 sts around foot opening. Bind off.

Finishing
Sew heel seam. Pin the sides of the shoe to the sole and ease in any excess. Sew together. Turn right side out. Make two 3 in. I-cord loops (see p. 28) for each shoe, 1 cream and 1 fawn.

Scarf
Using size 5 knitting needles and tweedy brown, cast on 24 sts.
Work 7 rows k1, p1 ribbing.
Continue in garter stitch (knit every row).
Work 4 rows cream, 4 rows fawn, and 4 rows olive green.
Work 190 rows tweedy brown.
Next row: Knit 12, turn, and slip rem 12 sts to a stitch holder.
Continue on these 12 sts and work 20 rows. Pick up rem 12 sts and re-join yarn. Work 20 rows on these sts. Now work across all 24 sts. You will have a large "buttonhole" in the middle of the scarf.
Work another 50 rows garter st.
Work 4 rows olive green, 4 rows fawn, then 4 rows cream.
Work 7 rows k1, p1 ribbing. Bind off in ribbing.
Tuck one end of scarf through the buttonhole.

Ladybug, Ladybug

Who doesn't love ladybugs? This beanie is a simple design in striking red and black. The ladybugs are knitted separately and stitched on once the hat is complete. Made in the same yarn as the hat, they don't require any additional scraps or colors of yarn, making this a good project for a beginner.

Sizes

To fit 18 months to 2 years (instructions for 3 to 4 years in parentheses)

Materials

1 x 50 g ball black DK yarn
1 x 50 g ball red wool DK yarn
Polyester fiberfill
Size 6 (4 mm) double-pointed
    knitting needles

Size 2 (3 mm) knitting needles
Yarn needle
Black stranded embroidery floss
Embroidery needle

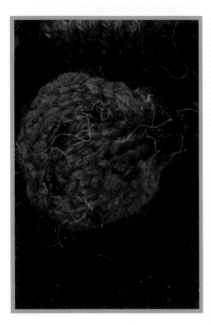

Hat

Using size 6 double-pointed knitting needles and black, cast on 92 (102) sts. Join into a ring, being careful not to twist the stitches.

Work 10 rounds st st (knit every round).

Break off black and join red.

Work in k2, p2 rib for 12 rounds.

Break off red and join black.

Round 23: Working in st st, dec 2 sts evenly on this round (90 / 100 sts). Cont in st st until work measures 6 (6 ½) in. cm from beg of rolled brim.

Crown Shaping

Work in alternating rounds of red and black:

Round 1: *K7 (8), k2tog, rep from * to end of round.

Round 2: Knit.

Round 3: *K6 (7), k2tog, rep from * to end of round.

Round 4: Knit.

Round 5: *K5 (6), k2tog, rep from * to end of round.

Continue decreasing in this pattern until 10 sts remain.

Break off yarn, thread through rem sts, pull up tightly, and fasten off.

Weave in all ends carefully on wrong side.

Ladybug

Using size 2 knitting needles and red, cast on 3 sts.

Row 1: Inc once in each of first two sts, k1 (5 sts).

Row 2 and all even rows: Purl.

Row 3: Kfb in first st, (k1, m1) twice, kfb in next st, k1 (9 sts).

Row 5: Kfb in first st, k3, m1, k1, m1, k2, kfb in next st, k1 (13 sts).

Row 7: Knit.

Row 9: (K1, sl1, k1, psso) twice, k1, (k2tog, k1) twice (9 sts).

Row 11: K1, sl2, k1, p2sso, k1, k2tog, slip stitch just made back on to left-hand needle, pass next st over it, then slip st back onto right-hand needle, k1 (5 sts).

Change to black for the head.

Row 12: Purl.

Row 13: K1, sl2, k1, p2sso, k1 (3 sts).

Row 14: Sl1, p2tog, psso. Fasten off.

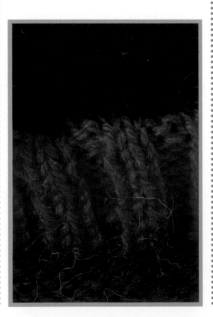

Underside

Using size 2 knitting needles and black, cast on 3 sts.

Row 1: Kfb in first two sts, k1 (5 sts).

Row 2 and all even rows: Purl.

Row 3: Kfb in first st, k2, kfb in next st, k1 (7 sts).

Rows 5 and 7: Knit.

Row 9: K1, sl1, k1, psso, k1, k2tog, k1 (5 sts).

Row 11: K1, sl2, k1, p2sso, k1 (3 sts).

Row 12: Sl1, p2tog, psso. Fasten off.

Make 7 ladybugs.

Finishing

Using 6 strands of black embroidery floss, embroider 5 spots on the upper side of each ladybug using bullion knots.

With wrong sides together, join upper body to underside, using very small stitches. When halfway around, insert a small amount of polyester fiberfill. Don't make the ladybugs too fat.

Sew one ladybug firmly to the top of the crown and place the other six at intervals around the hat.

Moonbeam

A colorful take on the traditional nightcap shape. This warm woolly hat will keep little heads cosy with its wide ribbed band, tapering shape and, for a bit of extra fun, some knitted balls attached to I-cords. This is a simple design knitted on two needles. You could also make it in a solid color—or go crazy and add more stripes.

Sizes

To fit 1–2 years (instructions for 3 to 4 years in parentheses)

- -

Materials

1 x 50 g ball red DK yarn
1 x 50 g ball white DK yarn
Small amounts of red and white baby yarn
Polyester fiberfill

Size 2 (2.75 mm) double-pointed knitting needles
Size 3 (3.25 mm) knitting needles
Size 6 (4 mm) knitting needles
Yarn needle

- -

Gauge

22 sts and 28 rows to 4 in. square, measured over st st on size 6 knitting needles.

Special Stitch

W&t (wrap and turn) [knit side]: Slip next stitch purlwise to right needle, then bring yarn to the front. Slip the same stitch back to the left needle, then return the yarn to the back and turn the work.

W&t (wrap and turn) [purl side]: Slip next stitch purlwise to right needle, then bring yarn to the back. Slip the same stitch back to the left needle, then return yarn to the front and turn the work.

Hat

Using size 3 knitting needles and red DK yarn, cast on 96 (108) sts. Work 20 rows in k1, p1 rib. Change to size 6 knitting needles. Join white DK yarn. Commence stripe pattern—2 rows red, 2 rows white—and work in st st until work measures 5 (5 ½) in. from beg, ending with a purl row.

Crown Shaping

Dec Row 1: *K22 (25), k2tog tbl, k2tog, k22 (25); repeat from * around. Work 3 rows st st without shaping.
Dec Row 2: *K21 (24), k2tog tbl, k2tog, k21 (24); repeat from * around. Work 3 rows st st without shaping.
Dec Row 3: *K20 (23), k2tog tbl, k2tog, k20 (23); repeat from * around. Work 3 rows st st without shaping. Cont decreasing in this pattern until 20 sts rem. Work another 3 rows without shaping.
Next row: K2tog all across row. Break off yarn, thread through rem sts, pull up tightly, and fasten off.

Knitted Balls

Using size 2 double-pointed knitting needles and baby yarn, cast on 12 sts.
Row 1: Knit.
Row 2: P10, w&t.
Row 3: K8, w&t.
Row 4: P6, w&t.
Row 5: K4, w&t.
Row 6: Purl.
Repeat these 6 rows 4 times. Bind off.

With right sides together, sew side seam halfway. Turn right side out and stuff firmly with fiberfill. Sew the remainder of the seam and then run a gathering thread around the top edge. Pull up firmly and fasten off. Do the same with the other end. Make 2 red balls and 2 white balls.

I-Cords

Using size 2 double-pointed knitting needles and red DK, cast on 3 sts. Make an I-cord as follows: *Knit all sts. *Do not turn.* Switch right-hand needle to left hand and pull sts to other end of needle. Pull yarn firmly around behind work, ready to knit into the first st again. Continue in this manner until each cord is the desired length. Sl1, k2tog, psso. Fasten off. Make 2 white I-cords, 4 in. and 5 in. long, and 2 red I-cords, 4 ½ in. and 5 ½ in. long.

Finishing

Press lightly if needed. Sew center back seam using backstitch or mattress stitch. Weave in any ends. Sew the white I-cords to the red balls and the red I-cords to the white balls. Sew the I-cords securely to the point of the hat.

Baby Jester

This little jester's cap looks complicated but really isn't too difficult to make. Knitted in the round, it divides at the crown and continues in two halves for the peaks. The colors are reversed in the peaks for added interest. Knitted balls and I-cords make this a fun little hat.

Size
To fit 6–9 months

Materials

2 x 50 g ball blue baby yarn
1 x 50 g ball cream baby yarn
Size 3 (3.25 mm) double-pointed knitting needles
Size 0 (2 mm) straight knitting needles

1 stitch holder
2 sets size 0 (2 mm) double-pointed knitting needles
Yarn needle
Small amount of polyester fiberfill

Special Stitch

W&t (wrap and turn) [knit side]: Slip next stitch purlwise to right needle, then bring yarn to the front. Slip the same stitch back to the left needle, then return the yarn to the back and turn the work.

W&t (wrap and turn) [purl side]: Slip next stitch purlwise to right needle, then bring yarn to the back. Slip the same stitch back to the left needle, then return yarn to the front and turn the work.

Hat

Using size 3 double-pointed knitting needles and blue, cast on 124 sts. Join into a ring, being careful not to twist the stitches. Mark the end of the round.

Work in k2, p2 rib for 32 rounds. The stripe pattern is made up of 7 rounds worked as follows:

Knit 4 rounds blue.
Knit 1 round cream.
Purl 1 round cream.
Knit 1 round cream.

Continue working striped pattern until work measures 7 in., ending with the last round of a blue stripe.

Crown Shaping

Place the first 62 st of the round on a stitch holder. Join the rem 62 stitches to work in rounds, marking the end of the round.

Work the 3 pattern rounds of cream as normal, decreasing 2 sts evenly on the first round. Knit another 4 rounds blue.

Dec round 1: With cream, *k2tog, k26, k2tog tbl; repeat from * to end of round.
Next round: With cream, purl.
Next round: With cream, knit. With blue, knit 4 rounds even.
Dec round 2: With cream, *k2tog, k24, k2tog tbl; repeat from * to end of round.
Next round: With cream, purl.
Next round: With cream, knit. With blue, knit 4 rounds even.
Dec round 3: With cream, *k2tog, k22, k2tog tbl; repeat from * to end of round.
Next round: With cream, purl.
Next round: With cream, knit. With blue, knit 4 rounds even. Continue decreasing in this pattern until 40 sts remain, then decrease only on every other white stripe until 12 stitches remain.

Next round: K2tog all around. Break off yarn, thread through remaining sts, pull up tightly, and, fasten off.

Place the stitches on the needle holder back on double-pointed needles and rejoin yarn. Complete as for the first side, reversing the colors.

Knitted Balls

With cream yarn and size 0 straight needles, cast on 12 sts.
Row 1: Knit.
Row 2: P10, w&t.
Row 3: K8, w&t.
Row 4: P6, w&t.
Row 5: K4, w&t.
Row 6: Purl.
Repeat these 6 rows 4 times. Bind off.

Make 6 I-cords, two 5 in. long to attach to the knitted balls and four 4 in. long to knot. Make half blue and half cream.

Finishing

Weave in all ends. Stitch up the opening on the crown between the two knitted points. Sew a blue ball to the longer cream I-cord and stitch this and two knotted I-cords to the end of one point. Repeat using the remaining I-cords and knitted ball on the other hat point.

Press lightly with a warm iron, but be careful not to flatten the ribbed pattern. Turn up the brim.

With right sides together, sew side seam halfway. Turn right side out and stuff firmly with fiberfill. Sew the remainder of the seam and then run a gathering thread around the top edge. Pull up firmly and fasten off. Do the same with the other end. Make 1 more with blue.

I-Cords

Using size 0 double-pointed knitting needles and blue yarn, cast on 3 sts. Make an I-cord as follows: *Knit all sts. *Do not turn.* Switch right-hand needle to left hand and pull sts to other end of needle. Pull yarn firmly around behind work, ready to knit into the first st again. Continue in this manner until the I-cord is the desired length. Sl1, k2tog, psso, fasten off.

Hello Sailor

A gorgeous floppy beret in fresh blue and white with a jaunty bow and a sparkle of beads on the top. This design is knitted in baby yarn so it is lightweight for mid-season and not too heavy for small heads. For the little ones it comes with matching booties, which have ribbed socks, a feature that makes them much more likely to stay on.

Sizes

Hat: To fit 12 months (instructions for 2 and 3 years in parentheses)
Slippers: To fit 12 months

Materials

I x 50 g ball French blue baby yarn
I x 50 g ball white baby yarn
Size 5 (3.75 mm) knitting needles
Size 3 (3.25 mm) knitting needles
Yarn needle

White stranded embroidery floss
Blue glass beads
Beading needle
White polyester thread

Hat

With size 5 knitting needles and white, cast on 64 (70, 76) sts.
Work 7 rows stockinette st.

Rows 8–11: Knit.

Rows 12 and 13: Knit in French blue.

Row 14: Knit in white.

Break off white. Continue in French blue.

Inc row 1: K5, [m1, k1, m1, k8 (9, 10)] 6 times, m1, k1, m1, k4 (78, 84, 90 sts).
Work 5 rows garter stitich.

Inc row 2: K6, [m1, k1, m1, k10 (11, 12)] 6 times, m1, k1, m1, k5 (92, 98, 104 sts).
Work 5 rows garter st.

Continue in this pattern, increasing 14 sts on each increase row (every 6th row), until there are 120 (140, 160) sts.

Next row: Purl.

Break off French blue. Join white and use for the remainder of the hat.

Dec row 1: K7 (8, 9), [k2tog, k1, k2tog, k12 (15, 18)], 6 times, k2tog, k1, k2tog, k6 (7, 8) (106, 126, 146 sts).
Beginning with a purl row, work 3 rows st st.

Dec row 2: K6 (7, 8), [k2tog, k1, k2tog, k10 (13, 16)], 6 times, k2tog, k1, k2tog, k5 (6, 7) (92, 112, 132 sts).
Work 3 rows st st.

Dec row 3: K5 (6, 7), [k2tog, k1, k2tog, k8 (11, 14)], 6 times, k2tog, k1, k2tog, k4, (5, 6) (78, 98, 118 sts).
Work 3 rows st st.

Continue in this pattern, decreasing 14 sts on each 4th row, until 22 (28, 34) sts rem.

Next row: K2tog across, (11, 14, 17 sts).

Next row: P1, *p2tog; rep from * to end.

Break off yarn, thread through rem sts, pull up tightly, and fasten off.

Finishing

With right sides together, sew center back seam using backstitch and appropriate colors. Fold the bottom edge of the hat to the inside and loosely sew in place. Be careful not to sew the hem too tightly or it may not fit the head. Thread the beading needle with a length of polyester thread and stitch the glass beads randomly to the crown of the beret. NOTE: Each bead should be sewn on individually and tied off; otherwise strands of thread will run across the inside of the hat and affect the stretch of the knitting.

Bow

Using size 3 knitting needles and French blue, cast on 21 sts.
Work 28 rows st st, commencing with a knit row. Bind off.

Fold in half, right sides together. Sew closed along one long and one short side and turn right side out. Sew closed. Wrap a length of yarn around the middle tightly a couple of times and fasten to form into a bow. Using 3 strands of white embroidery floss, make polka dots with bullion knots. Each bullion knot will need 16–18 wraps. Secure the bow to the front of the beret.

hello sailor **43**

Slippers

Sole

Using size 3 knitting needles and French blue, cast on 3 sts.

Row 1: Knit.

Row 2: Kfb in first st, k1, kfb in last st (5 sts).

Row 3: Kfb, k3, kfb (7 sts).

Row 4: Knit.

Row 5: Kfb, k5, kfb (9 sts).

Row 6: Kfb, k7, kfb (11 sts).

Row 7: Knit.

Row 8: Kfb, k9, kfb (13 sts).

Work another 28 rows in garter stitch without shaping.

Dec row 1: K2tog, knit to last 2 sts, k2tog.

Next row: Knit.

Repeat these two rows until 5 sts rem.

Top of Slipper

Row 1: Kfb in first 4 sts, k1 (9 sts).

Row 2 and all even rows: Purl.

Row 3: [K1, kfb in each of next 2 sts, k1], twice, k1 (13 sts).

Row 5: [K2, kfb in next 2 sts, k2] twice, k1 (17 sts).

Row 7: K3, kfb in next st, k8, kfb in next st, k4 (19 sts).

Row 9: Knit.

Row 10: [P2, kfb] twice, p6, [kfb, p2] twice, p1 (23 sts).

Work another 14 rows in stockinette stitch without shaping.

Row 25: K10, slip these sts to a stitch holder or piece of scrap yarn. Bind off next 3 sts, k10 (10 sts rem on needle).

Row 26 (first side) and every alternate row: Purl.

Row 27: K1, k2tog, k7.

Row 29: K1, k2tog, k6.

Row 31: K1, k2tog, k5.

Work another 15 rows without shaping. Bind off.

Take up sts from stitch holder; rejoin yarn at end of row.

Row 26 (second side) and every alternate row: Purl.

Row 27: K7, ssk, k1.

Row 29: K6, ssk, k1.

Row 31: K5, ssk, k1.

Work another 15 rows without shaping. Bind off.

Sock

Using size 3 knitting needles and white, pick up and knit 41 sts around foot opening.

Work 20 rows k1, p1 rib. Break off white and join blue. Work 3 rows in k1, p1, rib. Bind off in rib.

Finishing

Using mattress stitch, join heel and sock seam. With right sides together, pin top of slipper to sole. Stitch all the way around. Turn right side out.

Bows

Using size 3 knitting needles and blue, cast on 14 sts. Work 20 rows st st, starting with a knit row. Bind off. Finish as for the hat. Attach one bow firmly to the top of each slipper.

Pearly Queen

Usually I wouldn't put buttons on a hat for a little one, in case they accidentally found their way into the child's mouth. However, because this hat is for babies, who are unlikely to remove buttons on their own, I indulged a flight of fancy in this confection. Made with very soft wool baby yarn, it is simple to make and will keep your little one's head snuggly warm.

Size

To fit 3–9 months

Materials

1 x 50 g ball cream baby yarn
20 tiny pale-pink buttons
100 tiny cream buttons
30 in. pink ribbon
Size 3 (3.25 mm) knitting needles

Dec row 3: K1, (p2tog, k2tog) to end (20 sts).
Break off yarn. Thread through rem sts, pull up tightly, and fasten off. Sew seam, reversing stitching on lower third to allow for turning up of brim.

Buttons

Sew pink buttons on the crown and cream ones lower down. Each button must be sewn on individually or the hat will be unable to stretch. Make sure all buttons are sewn on very firmly. Turn up brim and thread ribbon through eyelets.

Hat

Using size 3 knitting needles, and cream, cast on 115 sts.
Work in k1, p1 ribbing until work measures 1 in, ending with an even-numbered row.
Eyelet row: K1, *yo, k2tog; rep from * to end.
Continue in ribbing until work measures 5 ½ in. from beg, ending with an even row.

Crown Shaping

Dec row 1: K1, p1, (k3tog, p1, k1, p1) 18 times, k3tog, p1, k1 (77 sts).
Work 3 rows in ribbing without shaping.
Dec row 2: K1, (p3tog, k1) 19 times (39 sts).
Work 1 row in ribbing without shaping.

Black Magic

Fun and sophisticated at the same time, this soft black hat is perfect for a special occasion. Made with black mohair and velvet ribbon, it has a luxury quality, but the polka dot knitted balls stop it from looking too grown up.

Size
To fit 18 months to 2 years

Materials
1 x 50 g ball black DK yarn
Small amount white DK yarn
Small amount black mohair DK yarn
30 in. of ³⁄₈ in. white velvet ribbon
Black and white stranded embroidery floss
Polyester fiberfill
Size 5 (3.75 mm) double-pointed knitting needles
1 pair of size 3 (3.25 mm) knitting needles
Yarn needle
Embroidery needle

Special stitches

Mb (make bobble): (K1, p1, k1, p1, k1) in next st; turn, purl next 5 sts; turn, knit next 5 sts; turn, purl next 5 sts; turn. Sl1 knitwise, k2tog twice, psso.

W&t (wrap and turn) [knit side]: Slip next stitch purlwise to right needle, then bring yarn to the front. Slip the same stitch back to the left needle, the return the yarn to the back and turn the work.

W&t (wrap and turn) [purl side]: Slip next stitch purlwise to right needle, then bring yarn to the back. Slip the same stitch back to the left needle, then return yarn to the front and turn the work.

Hat

Using size 5 double-pointed knitting needles and black mohair, cast on 92 sts on 3 needles.

Rounds 1–10: Knit.
Break off mohair and join regular black yarn.

Rounds 11–23: *K2, p2; rep from * to end.

Round 24: Knit, decreasing 2 sts evenly (90 sts).

Round 25: Knit.

Round 26: K1, *yo twice, k2tog; rep from * to end of round.

Round 27: Knit, dropping the second wrap of each yo twice from previous rnd off the needle as you knit.

Continue in st st until work measures 5 in. from rolled-up brim.

Next round: Purl.
Work 2 rounds st st.

Bobble round: *K4, mb; rep from * to end of round.
Work another 2 rounds st st.

Next round: Purl.
Work 3 rounds st st. Break off black and join white.

Crown Shaping

Round 1: *K7, k2tog; rep from * to end (80 sts).

Round 2 and all even rounds: Knit.

Round 3: *K6, k2tog; rep from * to end (70 sts).

Round 5: *K5, k2tog; rep from * to end (60 sts).

Continue in this pattern of decreasing until 20 sts remain. Break off yarn. Thread through rem sts, pull up tightly, and fasten off.

Finishing

Thread velvet ribbon through the eyelet holes and tie into a bow. Attach the balls to the top of the hat, securing firmly. Weave in all ends.

Knitted Balls

Using size 3 needles and black, cast on 12 sts.

Row 1: Knit.

Row 2: P10, w&t.

Row 3: K8, w&t.

Row 4: P6, w&t.

Row 5: K4, w&t.

Row 6: Purl.

Repeat these 6 rows 4 times. Bind off. Using 3 strands of white embroidery floss, make a bullion knot with 18 to 20 wraps anywhere on the knitted ball. Form into a circle. Secure with a couple of tiny stitches so it maintains a circular shape. Work several more bullion knots at random over the knitted piece.

With right sides together, sew side seam halfway. Turn right side out and stuff firmly with fiberfill. Sew the remainder of the seam and then run a gathering thread around the top edge. Pull up firmly and fasten off. Do the same with the other end. Make 5 balls in all, 3 in black with white polka dots and 2 in white with black polka dots.

Cotton Candy

A lovely pastel beanie in the colors of cotton candy, with a rolled mohair brim and kid mohair flowers that give it a very luxurious feel. It is perfect for the little princess who loves all things pink and flowery. If you use the pearl seed beads in the centers of the flowers, be sure to sew them on very securely so they can't be pulled or bitten off.

Size
To fit 18 months to 2½ years

Materials
1 x 50 g ball cream DK yarn
1 x 50 g ball pink DK yarn
Small amount pale pink mohair DK yarn
25 g ball Rowan Kid Silk Haze in pink
Pearl glass seed beads
Size 5 (3.75 mm) double-pointed knitting needles
Three size 1 (2.25 mm) double-pointed knitting needles
Yarn needle

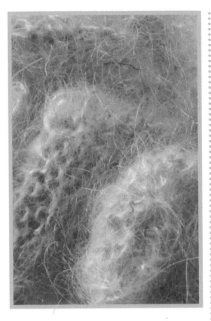

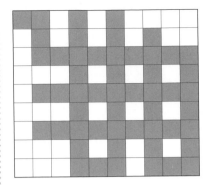

Special Stitches

Mb (make bobble): (K1, p1, k1, p1, k1) in next st; turn, purl next 5 sts; turn, knit next 5 sts; turn, purl next 5 sts; turn. Sl1 knitwise, k2tog twice, psso.

Hat

Using size 5 double-pointed needles and pale pink mohair, cast on 90 sts. Join to work in round, being careful not to twist sts.

Rounds 1–10: Knit.

Break off pale pink mohair and join cream.

Rounds 11–22: *K1, p1; repeat from * to end of round.

Rounds 23–24: Knit.

Join pink.

Rounds 25–33: Working with pink and cream, follow the chart above, repeating the 9 sts of the chart a total of 10 times on each round. Always carry the yarn not in use along the back of the work.

Rounds 34–36: With cream, knit.

Round 37: With pink, knit.

Round 38: With pink, purl.

Rounds 39–40: With cream, knit.

Round 41 (bobble round): *K4 with cream, mb with pink; repeat from * to end of round.

Rounds 43–44: With cream, knit.

Round 45: With pale pink, knit.

Round 46: With pale pink, purl.

Rounds 47–48: With cream, knit.

Rounds 49–52: Repeat rounds 45–48.

Crown Shaping

Break off pale pink and continue in cream for rest of hat.

Round 53: *K7, k2tog; repeat from * to end of round (80 sts).

Round 54 and all even rounds: Knit.

Round 55: *K6, k2tog; repeat from * to end of round (70 sts).

Round 57: *K5, k2tog; repeat from * to end of round (60 sts).

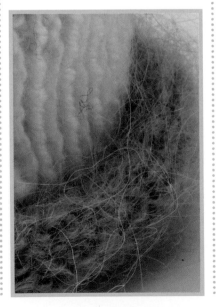

Finishing

Weave in all ends. Attach flowers to crown and sides of hat as desired.

Continue decreasing in this pattern until 20 sts remain.

Break off yarn. Thread end through rem sts, pull up tightly, and fasten off.

Flowers

Make a separate small ball of pale pink Kid Silk Haze, as these flowers are begun in two parts. To make a petal, using size 1 double-pointed knitting needles, cast on 3 sts. Using the separate ball of yarn and same needles, cast on 3 sts.

Row 1: (right side) K1, inc twice in next st, k1. Rep with other set of sts (5 sts in each set).

Row 2: Purl each set.

Row 3: K1, m1, k3, m1, k1. Rep with other set of sts (7 sts in each set).

Row 4: Join the 2 sets together by purling them together side by side

with the same ball of yarn as follows: p6, p2tog, p6.

Row 5: K1, m1, k11, m1, k1 (15 sts).

Rows 6 and every even row: Purl.

Row 7: K6, sl2, k1, p2sso, k6 (13 sts).

Row 9: K5, sl2, k1, p2sso, k5 (11 sts).

Row 11: Ssk, k2, sl2, k1, p2sso, k2, k2tog (7 sts).

Row 13: Ssk, sl2, k1, p2sso, k2tog (3 sts).

Row 14: Purl.

Leave these 3 sts on a spare needle. Make three more petals for each flower, setting aside each petal on the spare needle. Run a thread tightly through the 12 sts at the bases of the 4 petals and tie off. Stitch the pearl bead securely in the center of the flower.

Make 5 flowers.

Feathered Fancy

This beanie is inspired by a 1920's cloche hat, with its domed shape and feathers and flower decoration. A ribbon trim gives an extra touch of whimsy. Simple stitches combine to make this hat easy to knit but spectacular to look at and wear.

Size
To fit 2–3 years

Materials
1 x 50 g ball purple DK yarn
Small amounts of DK yarn in
   bright pink, light pink (LP),
   dark pink (DP), dark purple,
   light purple, and cream
40 in. of ⅜ in. bright pink ribbon

3 feathers
Size 6 (4 mm) double-pointed knitting needles
Yarn needle
Size D-3 (3.25 mm) crochet hook

Hat

Using size 6 double-pointed knitting needles and dark purple, cast on 92 sts. Join into a ring, being careful not to twist the sts.

Rounds 1–10: Knit.
Join bright pink.
Round 11: *K2 with purple, p2 with bright pink; repeat from * around.
Rounds 12–24: Repeat round 11.
Break off bright pink.
Round 25: Knit, decreasing 2 sts evenly on over round.
Round 26: Purl.
Round 27: Knit.
Round 28: Purl.
Round 29 (eyelet round): *Yo twice, k2tog; repeat from * around.
Round 30: Knit, dropping the second wrap of each yo twice from prev rnd as you go.

Round 31: Purl.
Round 32: Knit.
Break off purple and join dark pink (DP) and light pink (LP).
Round 33: *K3 with DP, k3 with LP; repeat from * around.
Round 34: Repeat round 33.
Round 35: *K3 with LP, k3 with DP; repeat from * around.
Round 36: Repeat round 35.
Rounds 37–38: Repeat rounds 33–34.
Break off LP and continue in DP.
Round 39: Knit.
Round 40: Purl.
Rounds 41–42: Repeat rounds 39–40.
Break off DP; join dark purple.
Rounds 43–45: Knit.
Round 46: Purl.
Break off purple; join DP and LP.

Rounds 47–50: Repeat rounds 33–36.
Break off LP and continue in DP.
Rounds 51–54: Repeat rounds 39–42.
Break off DP and join purple.

Crown Shaping
Round 55: *K7, k2tog; rep from * to end of round (80 sts).
Round 56 and every even round: Knit.
Round 57: *K6, k2tog; rep from * to end of round (70 sts).
Round 59: *K5, k2tog; rep from * to end of round (60 sts).
Continue decreasing in this pattern until 10 sts remain. Break off yarn, thread through rem sts, pull up tightly, and fasten off. Weave in all ends on wrong side.

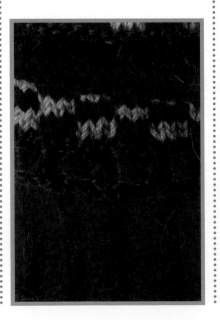

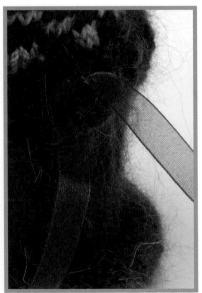

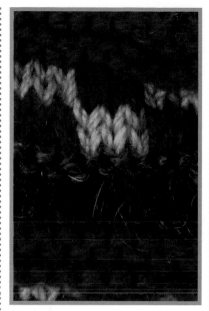

Finishing

Sew the roses securely to the crown around the feathers.
Weave in any loose ends.

Thread the ribbon through the eyelet holes, then tie in a generous bow.

Feather Bases

With size 6 needles, cast on 8 sts.
Work 16 rows in garter stitch. Bind off.
Make 3: 1 in cream, 1 in light purple, and 1 in light pink.

Wrap each feather base firmly around the base of a feather, starting at the cast on end. Sew in place.
Sew securely to the center of the hat, making sure the feathers stand upright. Weave in any loose ends.

Crochet Roses

With a size D-3 crochet hook, ch 48.
Skip first 1 ch, tr in next 13 ch, hdc in last ch.
Row 2: Ch 3, turn. Skip first st, work 3 dc in each tr to last 2 sts, sc in next st, sl st in last st.
Fasten off.
Starting at the end with the sl st, roll up the rose, securing it with small stitches at the base.
Make 3: 1 in cream, 1 in light purple, and 1 in light pink.

Bluebells and Cockleshells

I love blue and wanted to use up lots of odds and ends of yarn that I had. This hat evolved as a result. This is an excellent project for using up half balls of yarn. To link it together I have used feather and fan lace.

Size

To fit 18 months to 2 years

Materials

25 g DK yarn of each of the following: pale blue, French blue, medium blue, and bright blue
Small amounts of baby yarn in the following colors: bright blue, pale blue, navy, green

Size 6 (4 mm) double-pointed knitting needles
Size 1 (2.25 mm) double-pointed knitting needles
Yarn needle

Special Instructions

Feather and fan lace pattern:
(8-round repeat)
Round 1: Knit.
Round 2: K1, *k2tog twice, (yo, k1) three times, yo, ssk twice, k1; rep from * to end.
Rounds 3–6: Repeat rounds 1–2 twice.
Round 7: Knit.
Round 8: Knit.

Hat

Using size 6 double-pointed knitting needles and pale blue, cast on 96 sts. Join into a ring, being careful not to twist sts.
Rounds 1–34: *K2, p2; rep from * to end of round.
Break off pale blue and join bright blue.

Round 35: Knit, increasing 1 st on this round (97 sts).
Round 36: Purl.
Round 37: Knit.
Join French blue.
Rounds 38–45: Work feather and fan pattern.
Break off French blue and join bright blue.
Round 46: Knit.
Round 47: Purl.
Round 48: Knit.
Join medium blue.
Rounds 49–56: Work feather and fan pattern.
Round 57: Knit, increasing 3 sts evenly on this round (99 sts).
Round 58: Purl.
Round 59: Knit.

Crown shaping

Work in alternate rounds of pale blue and bright blue.
Round 60: *K7, k2tog; rep from * to end of round (88 sts).
Round 61: Knit.
Round 62: *K6, k2tog; rep from * to end of round (77 sts).
Round 63: Knit.
Round 64: *K5, k2tog; rep from * to end of round (66 sts).
Continue decreasing in this pattern until 11 sts remain.
Break off yarn, thread through rem sts, pull up tightly, and fasten off. Weave in all ends on wrong side.

Cornflowers

Make 3.
Use baby yarn—pale blue and dark blue for the center of the flower, and bright blue for the outer petals.
Using size 1 needles and dark blue, cast on 4 sts.
Row 1: (right side) With pale blue, k3 (1 st left unworked).
Row 2: With yarn at back, sl1 pwise, k2.
Rows 3–4: With dark blue, knit.
Repeat rows 1–4 nine times, then work rows 1–3 once more.
Bind off with dark blue.

Outer Petals

With right side facing and using bright blue, pick up and knit 22 sts along the long edge of the center piece.

Row 1: Inc in every st (44 sts).
Row 2: *Cast on 3 sts. Bind off 5 sts. Place last st back on left hand needle and rep from * to end, ending by binding off 4 sts.

Finishing

Join the ends of the piece to form a ring and gather the shorter edge tightly. Pin out the petals and stem block, if necessary. Attach the cornflowers evenly around the crown of the hat.

Bluebells

Using size 1 knitting needles and baby yarn, cast on 15 sts.
Row 1: (right side) Knit.
Row 2: Purl.
Row 3: (K2tog, yo) 7 times, k1.

Rows 4–6: Work in stockinette stitch, beginning with a purl row.
Row 7: Join hem: Insert right-hand needle in next st, then in back loop of corresponding st of cast-on row; k2tog. Repeat across.
Rows 8–12: Work in stockinette stitch, beginning with a purl row.
Row 13: (Sl2, k1, p2sso) 5 times.
Row 14: Purl.
Break off yarn, thread through rem sts, pull up tightly, and fasten off. Make 6 in bright blue and 2 in pale blue.

I-Cord Stem

Make stems all slightly different lengths.
With size 1 double-pointed knitting needles and green, cast on 3 sts. Make an I cord as follows: *Knit all sts. *Do not turn.* Switch right-hand

needle to left hand and pull sts to other end of needle. Pull yarn firmly around behind work, ready to knit into the first st again. Repeat from * until stem is the desired length. Sl1, k2tog, psso. Break yarn and draw end through rem st to fasten off.

Finishing

Leave a ¹/₂ in. tail when cutting the I-cord from the ball of yarn. Fray this end and insert it into the center of the bluebell, carefully enclosing it. Stitch the bluebell closed using an invisible seam. The stem will be enclosed in the bottom of the bluebell, with the frayed end peeping out of the top. Attach the other ends of the bluebell stems to the top of the hat, around the cornflowers.

Butterfly

Three butterflies adorn this hat, and a row of bobbles below the ribbed band give the hat a playful look. Vary the colors according to your child's favorites.

Size
To fit 18 months to 2 years

Materials
1 x 50 g ball purple DK yarn
1 x 50 g ball cream flecked DK yarn
1 x 50 g ball variegated pink, aqua
   and orange DK yarn
Small amounts of purple and pink
   baby yarn for the butterflies
Size 6 (4 mm) double-pointed
   knitting needles

Size 0 (2 mm) double-pointed
   knitting needles
Size 1 (2.25 mm) knitting needles
Polyester fiberfill
Yarn needle

Special stitches

Mb (make bobble): (K1, p1, k1, p1, k1) in next st; turn, purl next 5 sts; turn, knit next 5 sts; turn, purl next 5 sts; turn. Sl1 knitwise, k2tog twice, psso.

W&t (wrap and turn) [knit side]: Slip next stitch purlwise to right needle, then bring yarn to the front. Slip the same stitch back to the left needle, then return the yarn to the back and turn the work.

W&t (wrap and turn) [purl side]: Slip next stitch purlwise to right needle, then bring yarn to the back. Slip the same stitch back to the left needle, then return yarn to the front and turn the work.

Hat

Using size 6 double-pointed knitting needles and variegated yarn, cast on 95 sts.

Round 1: Knit.

Round 2: K2, *mb, k5, rep from * to last 3 sts, k3.

Round 3: Knit, decreasing 5 sts evenly on this round.
Break off variegated yarn; join purple yarn.

Rounds 4–18: *K1, p1; rep from * to end of round.

Round 19: With purple, knit.

Round 20: With variegated yarn, purl.

Round 21: With variegated yarn, knit.
Join cream.

Round 22: *K1 cream, k2 purple; repeat from * to end of round.

Round 23: *K2 cream, k1 purple; repeat from * to end of round.

Round 24: Repeat round 23.

Rounds 25–27: Repeat rounds 22–24.

Round 28: With variegated yarn, purl.

Round 29: With variegated yarn, knit. Break off variegated yarn.

Rounds 30–46: With cream, knit. Break off cream; join variegated yarn.

Round 47: Knit.

Round 48: Purl.

Round 49: Knit.

Round 50: Purl.

Crown Shaping

Work in alternating rounds of purple and variegated yarn.

Round 51: *K7, k2tog; rep from * to end of round (80 sts).

Round 52: Knit.

Round 53: *K6, k2tog; rep from * to end of round (70 sts).

Round 54: Knit.

Round 55: *K5, k2tog; rep from * to end of round (60 sts).
Continue decreasing in this pattern until 10 sts remain.
Break off yarn, thread through rem sts, pull up tightly, and fasten off. Weave in all ends on wrong side.

Butterfly

Make the butterflies from purple and pink baby yarn, using size 0 needles.

Lower Wing

Cast on 12 sts.
Row 1: (right side) K2, (p2, k1) 3 times, k1.
Row 2: K1, (p1, k2) 3 times, p1, k1.
Row 3: K2, (p2tog, k1) 3 times, k1 (9 sts).
Row 4: K1, (p1, k1) 4 times.
Row 5: K1, sl2, k1, p2sso, p1, sl2, k1, p2sso, k1 (5 sts).
Row 6: K1, (p1, k1) twice.
Row 7: K1, sl2, k1, p2sso, k1 (3 sts). Break off yarn; leave sts on a spare needle.
Make 2 lower wings for each butterfly.

Upper Wing

Cast on 12 sts.
Row 1: (right side) K2, (p2, k1) 3 times, k1.
Row 2: K1, (p1, k2) 3 times, p1, k1.
Rows 3–4: Repeat rows 1–2.
Row 5: K2, (p2tog, k1) 3 times, k1 (9 sts).
Row 6: K1, (p1, k1) 4 times.
Row 7: K2, (p1, k1) 3 times, k1.
Row 8: Repeat row 6.
Row 9: K1, sl2, k1, p2sso, p1, sl2, k1, p2sso, k1 (5 sts).
Row 10: K1 (p1, k1) twice.
Row 11: K1, sl2, k1, p2sso, k1 (3 sts). Break off yarn; leave sts on a spare needle.
Make 2 upper wings for each butterfly.

Body

Cast on 6 sts.
Bind off knitwise.

Assembly

Place the wings right sides together, lining up the pair of upper wings and the pair of lower wings on 2 needles, and then use the 3rd needle to bind them off together knitwise. Press wings lightly. Sew body to the top of the wings and use the yarn ends to make antennae. Make 3 butterflies in different shades.

To Finish

Sew the butterflies to the sides of the hat at even intervals. Add more if you like, or use slightly thicker yarn to make them bigger.

Knitted Ball

Using size 1 knitting needles and purple, cast on 12 sts.
Row 1: Knit.
Row 2: P10, w&t.
Row 3: K8, w&t.
Row 4: P6, w&t.
Row 5: K4, w&t.
Row 6: Purl.
Repeat these 6 rows 4 times. Bind off.
With right sides together, sew side seam halfway. Turn right side out and stuff firmly with fiberfill. Sew the remainder of the seam and then run a gathering thread around the top edge. Pull up firmly and fasten off. Do the same with the other end. Sew securely to the top of the crown.

Polka Dots

This is a simple beanie, suitable for a boy or a girl. If you make it for a boy, just omit the ribbon bow. The beanie is topped with red and white knitted balls and I-cords. For a plainer look you could leave these off.

Size
To fit 2–3 years

Materials
2 x 50 g balls of red DK yarn
1 x 50 g ball of white DK yarn
1 yd of ³/₈ in. white velvet ribbon
Size 6 (4 mm) double-pointed
    knitting needles

Size 2 (2.75mm) double-pointed
    knitting needles
Yarn needle
Polyester fiberfill

Special Stitches

Mb (make bobble): (K1, p1, k1, p1, k1) in next st; turn; purl next 5 sts; turn, knit next 5 sts; turn, purl next 5 sts; turn. Sl1 knitwise, k2tog twice, psso.

W&t (wrap and turn) [knit side]: Slip next stitch purlwise to right needle, then bring yarn to the front. Slip the same stitch back to the left needle, then return the yarn to the back and turn the work.

W&t (wrap and turn) [purl side]: Slip next stitch purlwise to right needle, then bring yarn to the back. Slip the same stitch back to the left needle, then return yarn to the front and turn the work.

Hat

Using size 6 double-pointed knitting needles and red, cast on 92 sts.

Rounds 1–32: *K2, p2; repeat from * to end of round.

Round 33: Knit, decreasing 2 sts evenly.

Rounds 34–35: Knit.

Round 36: Purl.

Round 37 (eyelet round): K1, *yo twice, k2tog; repeat from * to end of round.

Round 38: Knit, dropping the second wrap of each yo twice from the prev round as you go.

Round 39: Purl.

Rounds 40–41: Knit.

Join white.

Round 42 (bobble round 1): *K2 with red, mb with white, k2 with red; repeat from * around.

Rounds 43–46: With red, knit.

Round 47 (bobble round 2): *K4 with red, mb with white; repeat from * around.

Rounds 48–51: With red, knit.

Rounds 52–61: Repeat rounds 42–51.

Crown Shaping

Round 62: *K7, k2tog; rep from * to end.

Round 63 and all odd rounds: Knit.

Round 64: *K6, k2tog; rep from * to end.

Round 66: *K5, k2tog; rep from * to end.

Continue in this pattern until 20 sts remain. Break off yarn. Thread through rem sts, pull up tightly, and fasten off.

Knitted Balls

Using size 2 knitting needles and red, cast on 12 sts.

Row 1: Knit.
Row 2: P10, w&t.
Row 3: K8, w&t.
Row 4: P6, w&t.
Row 5: K4, w&t.
Row 6: Purl.

Repeat these 6 rows 4 times. Bind off.

With right sides together, sew side seam halfway. Turn right side out and stuff firmly with fiberfill. Sew the remainder of the seam and then run a gathering thread around the top edge. Pull up firmly and fasten off. Do the same with the other end. Make two red and white striped balls and one red ball. (To make the red ball, leave out the white stripes.)

I-Cords

Using size 2 double-pointed knitting needles, cast on 3 sts.

Make an I-cord as follows: *Knit all sts. *Do not turn.* Switch right-hand needle to left hand and pull sts to other end of needle. Pull yarn firmly around behind work, ready to knit into the first st again. Repeat from * until the cord is 2 1/2 in. long. Sl1, k2tog, psso. Fasten off.

Make 3 white and 3 red I-cords.

Finishing

Weave in all ends. Attach knitted balls and I-cords to the top of the hat. Turn up brim. Thread ribbon through eyelet holes and tie in a bow.

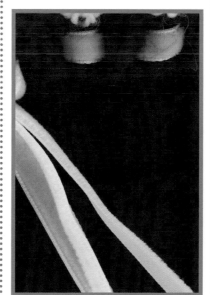

Chasing Rainbows

This bright and colorful beanie looks more complicated than it actually is. Made up of horizontal and vertical stripes, it also features decorative bobbles and some I-cord flourishes on top.

Size
To fit 12–18 months

Materials
1 x 50 g ball purple DK yarn
1 x 50 g ball bright pink DK yarn
Small amounts of DK yarn in bright green, orange, red, bright blue, and pale pink

Size 6 (4 mm) double-pointed knitting needles
Size 2 (3 mm) double-pointed knitting needles
Yarn needle

Special Stitches

Mb (make bobble): (K1, p1, k1, p1, k1) in next st; turn, purl next 5 sts; turn, knit next 5 sts; turn, purl next 5 sts; turn. Sl1 knitwise, k2tog twice, psso.

Hat

Using size 6 double-pointed knitting needles and purple, cast on 92 sts. Join into a ring, being careful not to twist the stitches.

Rounds 1–2: *K2, p2; rep from * to end of round. Join bright pink.

Round 3: *K2 pink, p2 purple; rep from * to end of round.

Rounds 4–16: Repeat round 3. Break off bright pink.

Round 17: Knit, decreasing 2 sts evenly.

Round 18: Purl.

Round 19: Knit.

Round 20: Purl.

Round 21: Knit.

Break off purple and join bright pink. Join white.

Rounds 22–23: Knit.

Round 24: *K4 with bright pink, mb with white; rep from * to end of round. Break off white.

Round 25: Knit.

Round 26: Purl.

Break off bright pink; join green.

Rounds 27–30: Repeat rounds 25–26.

Break off green; join blue.

Rounds 31–34: Repeat rounds 25–26.

Break off blue; join orange.

Rounds 35–38: Repeat rounds 25–26.

Break off orange; join red.

Rounds 39–42: Repeat rounds 25–26.

Break off red; join bright pink.

Rounds 43–44: Repeat rounds 25–26.

Rounds 45–46: Knit.

Join white.

Round 47: Repeat round 24.

Break off bright pink.

Round 48: Knit.

Round 49: Purl.

Round 50: Knit.

Crown Shaping

Work in alternating rounds of bright pink and purple.

Round 51: *K7, k2tog; rep from * to end of round.

Round 52: Knit.

Round 53: *K6, k2tog; rep from * to end of round.

Round 54: Knit.

Round 55: *K5, k2tog; rep from * to end of round.

Continue in this pattern until 10 sts remain.

Finishing

Knot the ends of three of the I-cords and sew the unknotted ends to the crown of the hat. Form the other three I-cords into loops and sew them to the crown of the hat in between the knotted I-cords.

Break off yarn, thread through rem sts, pull up tightly, and fasten off. Weave in all ends carefully on wrong side.

I-Cords

Using size 2 double-pointed needles, cast on 3 sts.

Make an I-cord as follows: *Knit all sts. Do not turn. Switch right hand needle to left hand and pull sts to other end of needle. Pull yarn firmly around behind work, ready to knit into the first st again. Repeat from * until I-cord is desired length.
Sl1, k2tog, psso. Fasten off.

Make six I-cords of varying lengths in different colors: green, bright pink, pale pink, orange, red, and blue.

Blue Top Knot

This jolly, bobbly creation is a great hat for boys and girls alike and is not too difficult to knit. The bobbles are knitted into the hat fabric and the colorful balls are knitted separately and attached at the end. Use any color scheme you like.

Size

To fit 2–4 years

Materials

2 x 50 g balls bright blue DK yarn
1 x 50 g ball cream DK yarn
Small amounts bright green and
   aqua DK yarn
Size 6 (4 mm) double-pointed
   knitting needles

Size 2 (2.75 mm) double-pointed
   knitting needles
Polyester fiberfill
Yarn needle

Special stitches

Mb (make bobble): (K1, p1, k1, p1, k1) in next st; turn, purl next 5 sts; turn, knit next 5 sts; turn, purl next 5 sts; turn. Sl1 knitwise, k2tog twice, psso.

W&t (wrap and turn) [knit side]: Slip next stitch purlwise to right needle, then bring yarn to the front. Slip the same stitch back to the left needle, then return yarn to the back and turn the work.

W&t (wrap and turn) [purl side]: Slip next stitch purlwise to right needle, then bring yarn to the back. Slip the same stitch back to the left needle, then return yarn to the front and turn the work.

Hat

Using size 6 double-pointed knitting needles and bright blue, cast on 92 (102) sts. Join to work in round, being careful not to twist the sts.

Rounds 1–32: *K2, p2; rep from * to end of round.

Round 33: [K43 (48), k2tog] twice; k2 (90 [100] sts).

Rounds 34–35: Knit.
Join cream.

Round 36 (bobble round 1): *K2 with blue, mb with cream, k2 with blue; repeat from * around.

Rounds 37–40: With blue, knit.

Round 41 (bobble round 2): *K4 with blue, mb with cream; repeat from * around.

Rounds 42–45: With blue, knit.

Rounds 46–55: Repeat rounds 36–45.

Break off cream.

Rounds 56–57: With blue, knit.

Crown Shaping

Round 58: *K7 (8), k2tog; rep from * to end of round (80 [90] sts).

Round 59: Knit.

Round 60: *K6 (7), k2tog; rep from * to end of round (70 [80] sts).

Round 61: Knit.

Round 62: *K5 (6), k2tog; rep from * to end of round (60 [70] sts).

Continue decreasing in this pattern until 10 sts remain.

Break off yarn, thread through rem sts, pull up tightly, and fasten off. Weave in all ends on the wrong side.

Knitted Balls

Using size 2 knitting needles, cast on 12 sts.

Row 1: Knit.

Row 2: P10, w&t.

Row 3: K8, w&t.

Row 4: P6, w&t.

into the first st again. Repeat from * until I-cord is desired length. Sl1, k2tog, psso. Fastern off.

Make 4 I-cords, each 6 in. long, to match the knitted balls.

Finishing

Knot the ends of the I-cords loosely. Sew the I-cords and knitted balls securely to the crown of the hat in a pleasing color pattern. Turn up ribbed brim.

Row 5: K4, w&t.

Row 6: Purl.

Rep these 6 rows 4 times. Bind off With right sides together sew side seam halfway. Turn right side out and stuff firmly. Sew the remainder of the seam and then run a gathering thread around the top edge. Pull up firmly and fasten off. Do the same at the other end.

Make 1 white, 1 green, 1 aqua, and 1 bright blue.

I-Cords

Using size 2 double-pointed needles, cast on 3 sts.

Make an I-cord as follows: *Knit all sts. *Do not turn.* Switch right-hand needle to left hand and pull sts to other end of needle. Pull yarn firmly around behind work, ready to knit

Cherry Ripe

This delightful cherry-topped hat will brighten up any cold winter's day. Knit as many or as few cherries as you like. For a simple effect, a single cherry on top would look beautiful. For a more playful look, add the full bunch of nine; it's worth the extra time.

Size
To fit 18 months to 2 years

Materials
1 x 50 g ball cream DK yarn
1 x 50 g ball variegated pink, red, and orange DK yarn
Small amounts of red and green DK yarn
25 g red baby yarn for cherries
Size 6 (4 mm) double-pointed knitting needles

Size 1 (2.25 mm) knitting needles
Size 2 (2.25 mm) double-pointed knitting needles
Size C-2 (2.75 mm) crochet hook
Polyester fiberfill
Yarn needle

Special Stitch

W&t (wrap and turn) [knit side]: Slip next stitch purlwise to right needle, then bring yarn to the front. Slip the same stitch back to the left needle, then return the yarn to the back and turn the work.

W&t (wrap and turn) [purl side]: Slip next stitch purlwise to right needle, then bring yarn to the back. Slip the same stitch back to the left needle, then return yarn to the front and turn the work.

Hat

Using size 6 double-pointed knitting needles and variegated yarn, cast on 92 sts. Join to work in round, being careful not to twist the stitches.

Rounds 1–32: *K2, p2; rep from * to end of round.

Break off variegated yarn and join cream.

Round 33: [K43 (48), k2tog] twice; k2 (90 sts).

Round 34: Knit.

Round 35: Purl.

Round 36: Knit.

Join red and green.

Rounds 37–38: *K3 green, k3 red, k3 cream; rep from * to end of round.

Rounds 39–40: *K3 cream, k3 green, k3 red; rep from * to end of round.

Rounds 41–42: *K3 green, k3 red, k3 cream; rep from * to end of round.

Break off red and green yarn.

Round 43: With cream, knit.

Round 44: Purl.

Rounds 45–54: Knit.

Round 55: Purl.

Round 56: Knit.

Join green.

Round 57: Knit using green.

Join red.

Round 58: Knit using red.

Round 59: Knit using green.

Break off green and red.

Round 60: Knit using cream.

Round 61: Purl using cream.

Crown Shaping

Work in alternating stripes of 1 round cream and 1 round variegated yarn.

Round 62: *K7, k2tog; rep from * to end of round.

Round 63: Knit.

Round 64: *K6, k2tog; rep from * to end of round.

Round 65: Knit.

Round 66: *K5, k2tog; rep from * to end of round.

Continue decreasing in this pattern until 10 sts remain.

Break off yarn, thread through rem sts, pull up tightly, and fasten off. Weave in all ends on wrong side.

Cherries

Using size 1 needles and red baby yarn, cast on 12 sts.

Row 1: Knit.
Row 2: P10, w&t.
Row 3: K8, w&t.
Row 4: P6, w&t.
Row 5: K4, w&t.
Row 6: Purl.

Rep these 6 rows 4 times. Bind off. With right sides together, sew side seam halfway. Turn right side out and stuff firmly. Sew the rest of the seam and then run a gathering thread around the top edge. Pull up firmly and fasten off. Do the same with the other end.
Make 9

Stems

Using a size C-2 crochet hook, ch 10. Fasten off. Sew a cherry to one end.

Leaves

Using size 2 double-pointed knitting needles and green, cast on 3 sts. Work an I-cord as follows: *Knit all sts. *Do not turn.* Switch right-hand needle to left hand and pull sts to other end of needle. Pull yarn firmly around behind work, ready to knit into the first st again. Repeat from * until I-cord stem measures 1 in. Now work forward and backward in rows, beginning the first row by switching the work to the left hand without turning and pulling the yarn around behind the work, as in the basic I-cord.

Row 1: K1, yo, k1, yo, k1.
Row 2 and all even rows: K1, p to last st, k1.
Row 3: K2, yo, k1, yo, k2.
Row 5: K3, yo, k1, yo, k3.
Row 7: K4, yo, k1, yo, k4.
Row 9: K5, yo, k1, yo, k5.
Row 11: Ssk, k9, k2tog.
Row 13: Ssk, k7, k2tog.
Row 15: Ssk, k5, k2tog.
Row 17: Ssk, k3, k2tog.
Row 19: Ssk, k1, k2tog.
Row 21: Sl1, k2tog, psso.

Fasten off and weave in ends.
Make 8.

Finishing

Sew the stems of 8 cherries to crown of hat. Do the same with leaves, arranging them between the cherries. With last cherry, twist crocheted stem tightly until curled. With red yarn, sew base of last cherry to center of crown. Weave in all ends on wrong side.

Strawberries and Cream

Cheer up a wintery day with this vibrant, fresh beanie.
Although the strawberries look tricky, they are really quite easy.
The beads are threaded onto the yarn first, rather than being
sewn on later. Make the hat first and set aside until the leaves
and strawberries are complete.

Size

To fit 18 months to 2 years

Materials

1 x 50 g ball cream DK yarn
1 x 50 g ball red DK yarn
1 x 50 g ball pink and orange
    variegated DK yarn
1 x 50 g ball bright green DK yarn
Small amount red baby yarn
Small amount bright green baby
    yarn
Size 5 (3.75 mm) double-pointed
    knitting needles

Size 2 (2.75 mm) double-pointed
    knitting needles
Size 1 (2.25 mm) double-pointed
    knitting needles
360 red glass seed beads
Needle for threading beads onto
    yarn
Yarn needle
Polyester fiberfill

Special Stitches

B1 (bead 1): Bring yarn to the front, slip the next st purlwise, slide bead along yarn so that it sits firmly against the knitted fabric, take yarn to back of work, ready to knit next st.

Mb (make bobble): (K1, p1, k1, p1, k1) in next st; turn, purl next 5 sts; turn, knit next 5 sts; turn, purl next 5 sts; turn. Sl1 knitwise, k2tog twice, psso.

Hat

Using size 5 double-pointed knitting needles and variegated yarn, cast on 90 sts.

Rounds 1–10: Knit.

Break off variegated yarn and join red yarn

Rounds 11–24: *K1, p1; rep from * to end of round.

Break off red; join variegated yarn.

Round 25: Knit.
Round 26: Purl.
Round 27: Knit.
Round 28 (bobble round): Join cream. *K4 with variegated yarn, mb with cream; repeat from * to end of round. Break off cream.
Rounds 29–30: Knit.
Round 31: Purl.
Break off variegated yarn; join red.
Rounds 32–37: Knit.
Break off red; join variegated yarn.
Round 38: Purl.
Rounds 39–40: Knit.
Rounds 41–48: Repeat rounds 28–35.
Break off red; join cream.

Crown Shaping

Round 49: *K7, k2tog; rep from * to end (80 sts).
Round 50 and all even rounds: Knit.
Round 51: *K6, k2tog; rep from * to end (70 sts).
Round 53: *K5, k2tog; rep from * to end (60 sts).
Continue decreasing in this pattern until 20 sts remain. Break off yarn. Thread through rem sts, pull up tightly, and fasten off.

Strawberries

Berry Body

Thread 36 beads onto red baby yarn. Using size 1 double-pointed knitting needles and red baby yarn with beads, cast on 3 sts.

Row 1: (wrong side) Kfb in first st, p1, kfb in last st (5 sts).
Row 2: (K1, b1) twice, k1.
Row 3: Kfb in first st, p3, kfb in last st (7 st).
Row 4: (K1, b1) to last st, k1.
Row 5: Kfb in first st, p5, kfb in last st (9 sts).
Row 6: Repeat row 4.
Row 7: Kfb in first st, p7, kfb in last st (11 sts).
Row 8: Repeat row 4.
Row 9: K1, p9, k1.
Row 10: K2, (b1, k1) to last st, k1.
Row 11: Repeat row 9.
Row 12: (K1, b1) to last st, k1.
Row 13: Repeat row 9.
Row 14: Repeat row 10.
Row 15: Repeat row 9.
Row 16: Repeat row 12.

Row 17: Ssk, (b1, k1) to last 3 sts, b1, k2tog (9 sts).
Row 18: K1, p7, k1.
Bind off.
Make 10 (makes 5 berries).

Calyx
Using size 1 double-pointed knitting needles and bright green baby yarn, cast on 8 sts.
Row 1: (wrong side) Bind off 5 sts, k2, turn (3 sts).
Row 2: Cast on 5 sts (8 sts).
Repeat rows 1 and 2 four times. Bind off.

Finishing
Sew two strawberry body pieces together with right sides together, leaving top open. Turn right side out. Stuff firmly with polyester fiberfill. Sew the calyx securely to the top of the strawberry.

Leaves
Using size 2 double-pointed knitting needles and bright green DK yarn, cast on 8 sts, then bind off 6 sts (2 sts rem).
Row 1: (right side) K1, M1, k1.
Row 2: Purl.
Row 3: K1, M1, k1, M1, k1.
Row 4 and all even rows to row 24: K1, p to last st, k1.
Row 5: K2, M1, k1, M1, k2.
Row 7: K3, M1, k1, M1, k3.
Row 9: K4, M1, k1, M1, k4.
Row 11: K5, M1, k1, M1, k5.
Row 13: Knit.
Row 15: Knit.
Row 17: K5, sl2, k1, p2sso, k5.
Row 19: K4, sl2, k1, p2sso, k4.
Row 21: K3, sl2, k1, p2sso, k3.
Row 23: K2, sl2, k1, p2sso, k2.
Row 24: Purl.
Row 25: K1, sl2, k1, p2sso, k1.
Row 26: Purl.
Row 27: Sl2, k1, p2sso. Fasten off.
Make 10.
Press leaves to flatten into shape.

Finishing
Attach the leaves fanning out from the center of the top of the hat and then sew the strawberries firmly on the top. Weave in ends.

Twist and Twirl

Turn heads with this twizzling number. Perfect for boys or girls—just change your color scheme to suit. The crown decorations are added when the hat is complete, and everything else is incorporated into the knitting as you go. This pattern provides a good opportunity to use up small amounts of leftover yarn.

Size
To fit 18 months to 2 years

Materials
1 x 50 g ball red DK yarn
1 x 50 g ball navy DK yarn
Small amounts DK yarn in eight bright colors
Set of 5 size 6 (4 mm) double-pointed knitting needles

Size 2 (2.75 mm) double-pointed knitting needles
Yarn needle
Polyester fiberfill

Special Stitches

Kt (knitted twirl): With contrasting color and extra double-pointed knitting needle, knit into next st and cast on 15 sts. Knit 2 rows on these sts in the contrasting color. Bind off 15 sts.

Mb (make bobble): (K1, p1, k1, p1, k1) in next st; turn, purl next 5 sts; turn, knit next 5 sts; turn, purl next 5 sts; turn. Sl1 knitwise, k2tog twice, psso.

W&t (wrap and turn) [knit side]: Slip next stitch purlwise to right needle, then bring yarn to the front. Slip the same stitch back to the left needle, then return yarn to the back and turn the work.

W&t (wrap and turn) [purl side]: Slip next stitch purlwise to right needle, then bring yarn to the back. Slip the same stitch back to the left needle, then return yarn to the front and turn the work.

Hat

Using size 6 double-pointed knitting needles and red DK yarn, cast on 90 sts. Join to work in round, being careful not to twist sts.

Rounds 1–32: *K1, p1; rep from * to end of round.

Break off red; join navy blue.

Round 33: Knit.

Round 34: Purl.

Round 35: Knit.

Round 36: Purl.

Round 37: Knit.

Round 38: *K8, kt (using a different contrasting color for each twirl); rep from * to end of round.

Rounds 39–40: Knit.

Round 41: Purl.

Round 42: Knit.

Round 43: Purl.

Round 44: Knit.

Round 45: Knit.

Round 46: Join bright green. *K4 with navy blue, mb with bright green; rep from * to end of round. Break off bright green.

Rounds 47–48: Knit.

Rounds 49–57: Repeat rounds 36–44.

Break off navy blue; join red.

Crown Shaping

Round 58: *K7, k2tog; rep from * to end of round (80 sts).

Round 59: Knit.

Round 60: *K6, k2tog; rep from * to end of round (70 sts).

Round 61: Knit.

Round 62: *K5, k2tog; rep from * to end of round (60 sts).

Continue decreasing in this pattern until 10 sts remain.

Break off yarn, thread through rem sts, pull up tightly, and fasten off. Weave in ends on wrong side.

Knitted Balls

Using size 2 knitting needles, cast on 12 sts.

Row 1: Knit.

Row 2: P10, w&t.

Row 3: K8, w&t.

Row 4: P6, w&t.

Row 5: K4, w&t.

Row 6: Purl.

Repeat these 6 rows 4 times. Bind off. With right sides together, sew side seam halfway. Turn right side out and stuff firmly with fiberfill. Sew the remainder of the seam and then run a gathering thread around the top edge. Pull up firmly and fasten off. Do the same with the other end.

I-Cord Loops

Using size 2 needles, cast on 3 sts. Make an I-cord as follows: *Knit all sts. *Do not turn.* Switch right-hand needle to left hand and pull sts to other end of needle. Pull yarn firmly around behind work, ready to knit into the first st again. Repeat from * until cord measures 4 in. Sl1, k2tog, psso; fasten off.

Join into a loop by stitching ends together.

Make 6 I-cords in various colors.

Finishing

Sew the I-cord loops and the knitted balls securely to the top of the hat. Weave in the ends on the wrong side.

Loopy Hat

This cheerful loopy hat knitted in varying shades of blue is perfect for keeping out the chill of a winter's day. Make the I-cord loops first, then set them aside to be knitted into the main body of the hat.

Size
To fit 12–18 months

- -

Materials
Assorted shades of blue DK yarn

Size 6 (4 mm) double-pointed
   knitting needles

Size 2 (2.75 mm) double-pointed
   knitting needles

Yarn needle

Stitch holders

Polyester fiberfill

- -

Special Stitches

Place loop: Put I-cord loop on left needle. Knit together with next st by knitting through the back "leg" of the I-cord loop and the back leg of the next stitch. Pull on I-cord just knitted to pull out any excess and tighten stitch just knit.

W&t (wrap and turn) [knit side]: Slip next stitch purlwise to right needle, then bring yarn to the front. Slip the same stitch back to the left needle, then return yarn to the back and turn the work.

W&t (wrap and turn) [purl side]: Slip next stitch purlwise to right needle, then bring yarn to the back. Slip the same stitch back to the left needle, then return yarn to the front and turn the work.

Make the loops and balls first.

I-Cord Loops

With size 2 double-pointed needles, cast on 3 sts. Make an I-cord as follows: *Knit all sts. *Do not turn.* Switch right-hand needle to left hand and pull sts to other end of needle. Pull yarn firmly around behind work, ready to knit into the first st again. Rep from * until I-cord measures 3 1/2 in. Sl1, k2tog, psso and leave rem st on stitch holder.
Make 30 in various colors.

Knitted Balls

With size 2 knitting needles, cast on 12 sts.

Row 1: Knit.
Row 2: P10, w&t.
Row 3: K8, w&t.
Row 4: P6, w&t.
Row 5: K4, w&t.
Row 6: Purl.
Repeat these 6 rows 4 times. Bind off. With right sides together, sew side seam halfway. Turn right side out and stuff firmly with fiberfill. Sew the remainder of the seam and then run a gathering thread around the top edge. Pull up firmly and fasten off. Do the same with the other end. Make 3 in different colors.

Hat

Using size 6 double-pointed knitting needles, cast on 80 sts evenly on 3 needles.
Rounds 1–30: *K2, p2; rep from * to end of round.
Round 31: Change to first stripe color; knit.
Round 32: Purl.
Round 33: Change to second stripe color; knit.
Round 34: Purl.
Round 35: Change to third stripe color; knit.
Round 36: Purl.
Break off third stripe color; join main hat color.
Rounds 37–40: Knit.
Round 41: K4, *place loop, k7; rep from * to end of rnd, using a different-colored I-cord each time and ending with k3.
Rounds 42–47: Knit.

Round 48: K7, *place loop, k7; rep from * to end of round.
Rounds 49–54: Knit.
Round 55: Repeat round 41.
Rounds 56–61: Knit.
Rounds 62–67: Repeat rounds 31–36.

Crown Shaping

Round 68: *K6, k2tog; rep from * to end (70 sts).
Round 69 and all odd rounds: Knit.
Round 70: *K5, k2tog; rep from * to end (60 sts).
Round 72: *K4, k2tog; rep from * to end (50 sts).
Continue decreasing in this pattern until 20 sts remain.
Break off yarn, thread through rem sts, pull up tightly, and fasten off. Weave in all ends. Sew the knitted balls securely to the top of the hat. Fold up brim.

Carnival

Keep out the winter chills and put a smile on the face of the lucky child who receives this cheerful hat. This hat is very textural, featuring bobbles, knitted-in twists and triangles, and a striped ribbed band. It's not a beginner's project, but the knitting is exciting and the end result very worthwhile.

Size

To fit 18 months to 2 years

Materials

1 x 50 g ball red DK yarn
1 x 50 g ball white DK yarn
1 x 50 g ball navy DK yarn
1 x 50 g ball medium blue DK yarn
1 x 50 g ball light blue DK yarn
Size 5 (3.75 mm) double-pointed
  knitting needles

Size 2 (2.75 mm) double-pointed
  knitting needles
1 spare needle
Yarn needle

Special Stitch

Mb (make bobble): (K1, p1, k1, p1, k1) in next st; turn, purl next 5 sts; turn, knit next 5 sts; turn, purl next 5 sts; turn. Sl1 knitwise, k2tog twice, psso.

Triangle Flaps

Cast on 9 stitches; divide evenly on 3 needles and join to work in round, being careful not to twist the stitches.

Round 1: Knit.
Round 2: *K1, kfb, k1; rep from * to end (12 sts).
Rounds 3–4: Knit.
Round 5: *K1, kfb twice, k1; rep from * to end (18 sts).
Rounds 6–7: Knit.
Round 8: *K1, kfb; rep from * to end (27 sts).

Rounds 9–10: Knit.
Round 11: Knit to last 2 sts, k2tog (26 sts).
Round 12: Divide sts evenly on to two needles. Holding needles parallel, knit each stitch from the front needle together with the corresponding stitch from the back needle. (You should end with 13 live sts.)
Run a gathering thread along the cast-on edge at the tip of the triangle. Pull up tightly and fasten off on the inside of the triangle.
Make 9 triangles: 4 light blue, 4 medium blue and 1 red. Set aside on spare needle.

Hat

Using size 5 double-pointed needles and navy, cast on 90 sts and distribute evenly on 3 needles. Join to work in round, being careful not to twist.

Rounds 1–10: Knit.
Join white.
Rounds 11–20: *K1 with navy, p1 with white; rep from * to end of round.
Break off navy and white and join medium blue.
Rounds 21–22: Knit.
Round 23 (triangle round): *K2tog, k3, k2tog, k4, k2tog, place triangle (see below); rep from * to end.
Placing triangles: Attach triangles to work by placing spare needle with live stitches of triangle on left side, parallel with stitches to be knit. Knit triangle stitches together with hat sts. Alternate triangle colors, ending with one red triangle.
Rounds 24–26: Knit.
Break off medium blue; join white.
Round 27: Knit.
Round 28: Purl.
Break off white; join navy.
Rounds 29–30: Repeat rounds 27–28.
Break off navy; join red.
Rounds 31–32: Knit.
Round 33: *K4, mb; rep from * to end of round.
Rounds 34–35: Knit.
Break off red; join navy.
Rounds 36–37: Repeat rounds 27–28.
Break off navy; join white.
Rounds 38–39: Repeat rounds 27–28.
Break off white; join medium blue.
Rounds 40–43: Knit.
Round 44: *Using knitted cast on, cast on 15 sts with white in next st;

cast off same 15 sts (twist made); with medium blue, k9; rep from * around, alternating twist colors between white, navy, and red (the 9 sts between twists remain medium blue). Break off all colors except medium blue. There will be 9 knitted twists in all, 3 of each color.

Rounds 45–47: Knit.

Break off medium blue; join white.

Rounds 48–49: Repeat rounds 27–28.

Break off white; join navy.

Rounds 50–51: Repeat rounds 27–28.

Break off navy; join red.

Round 52: Knit.

Join white (do not break off red).

Crown Shaping

Round 53 (setup round for crown shaping): *K1 red, k1 white; rep from * to end of round.

Throughout decreasing, knit red stitches with red and white with white to maintain vertical stripes.

Round 54: *K7, sl2, k1, p2sso; rep from * to end of round (72 sts).

Rounds 55–56: Knit.

Round 57: *K5, sl2, k1, p2sso; rep from * to end of round (54 sts).

Rounds 58–59: Knit.

Round 60: *K3, sl2, k1, p2sso; rep from * to end of round (36 sts).

Rounds 61–62: Knit.

Round 63: *K1, sl2, k1, p2sso; rep from * to end of round (18 sts).

Break off yarn, thread through rem sts, pull up tightly, and fasten off.

I-Cords

With size 2 double-pointed needles, cast on 3 sts. Make an I-cord as follows: *Knit all sts. *Do not turn.* Switch right-hand needle to left hand and pull sts to other end of needle. Pull yarn firmly around behind work, ready to knit into the first st again. Repeat from * until I-cord measures 3 inches. Sl1, k2tog, psso. Fasten off. Make 5, one in each color.

Finishing

Loosely knot the ends of the I-cords. Sew the unknotted ends securely to the crown of the hat. Weave in all ends on the wrong side.

Socks on The Washing Line

Combine your passions for knitting socks and hats with this whimsical design. Tiny socks are strung on a washing line around the hat and one sock sits on top, surrounded by buttoned I-cord loops. If you have knitted socks before, you will easily be able to manage these scaled-down versions.

Size

To fit 2–4 years

Materials

2 x 50 g balls of red DK yarn
Small amount of sock yarn
Small amount of red sock or baby yarn
15 small red buttons
Size 5 (3.75 mm) double-pointed knitting needles

Size 1 (2.25 mm) double-pointed knitting needles
Polyester fiberfill
Yarn needle
Red sewing thread
Sewing needle

Hat

Using size 5 double-pointed knitting needles and red DK yarn, cast on 90 sts.

Rounds 1–28: *K1, p1; rep from * to end of round.

Rounds 29–33: Knit.

Round 34: Purl.

Rounds 35–46: Knit.

Round 47: Purl.

Rounds 48–52: Knit.

Round 53: Purl.

Crown Shaping

Round 54: *K7, k2tog; rep from * to end (80 sts).

Round 55 and every odd round: Knit.

Round 56: *K6, k2tog; rep from * to end (70 sts).

Round 58: *K5, k2tog; rep from * to end (60 sts).

Continue decreasing in this pattern until 20 sts remain. Break off yarn. Thread through rem sts, pull up tightly, and fasten off.

I-Cord Clothesline

Using size 1 double-pointed knitting needles, cast on 2 sts. Make an I-cord as follows: *Knit all sts. *Do not turn.* Switch right-hand needle to left hand and pull sts to other end of needle. Pull yarn firmly around behind work, ready to knit into the first st again. Rep from * until I-cord is long enough to fit loosely around the hat. Sl1, k1, psso; fasten off.

Socks

With size 1 double-pointed knitting needles and sock yarn, cast on 24 sts. Join to work in round, being careful not to twist sts.

Rounds 1–5: *K1, p1; rep from * to end of round.

Rounds 6–12: Knit.

Divide for Heel

K12. Slip these 12 sts to one needle and remaining 12 sts to another needle.

Working with the 12 sts just knitted, turn and begin working back and forth in rows.

Row 1: Sl1, purl to end.

Row 2: *Sl1, k1; rep from * to end.

Rows 3–6: Repeat rows 1–2.

Row 7: Repeat row 1.

Turn Heel
Row 8: K8, turn.
Row 9: P4, turn.
Row 10: K3, ssk, k1, turn.
Row 11: P4, p2tog, p1, turn.
Row 12: K5, ssk, k1, turn.
Row 13: P6, p2tog, p1, turn.
Row 14: K4. Place marker (this is the new beginning of round).

Gusset
Round 15 (setup round): K4, pick up and knit 6 sts along heel flap. Place marker. Knit the 12 sts from second needle (the sts set aside before). Place marker. Pick up and knit 6 sts on other side of heel flap; k4.
Round 16: Knit.
Round 17: Knit to last 3 sts before first marker; k2tog, k1. Slip marker. K12. Slip marker. Ssk, k1, knit to end.

Rounds 18–23: Repeat rounds 16–17 (24 sts rem after round 23).
Rounds 24–26: Knit.

Toe Decreasing
Round 27: Knit.
Round 28: Knit to last 3 sts before first marker; k2tog, k1. Slip marker. K1, ssk; knit to last 3 sts before second marker; k2tog, k1. Slip marker. K1, ssk, knit to end of rnd.
Repeat rounds 27–28 until 8 sts rem. Break off yarn, thread through rem sts, pull tightly, and fasten off. Weave in ends.

Make 6 socks.

I-Cord Loops
Using size 5 double-pointed knitting needles and red DK yarn, cast on 3 sts. Make an I-cord as follows: *Knit all sts. *Do not turn.* Switch right-hand needle to left hand and pull sts to other end of needle. Pull yarn firmly around behind work, ready to knit into the first st again. Rep from * until I-cord measures 3 ½ in. Sl1, k2tog, psso. Fasten off.
Sew the ends together to form a loop and sew a button over the join. Make 10.

Finishing
Sew the washing line to the hat at 5 points on the second purl row. At each of these points, attach a knitted sock, sewing on a button where the sock is attached. Make sure all the socks face the same direction. Lightly stuff the sixth sock and sew it closed along the top of the ribbing. Sew to the center of the top of the hat. Sew the buttoned loops evenly around the top of the hat.
Weave in all ends.

Blooming Gorgeous

I wanted the flowers on this hat to look like they were coming out of the crown. To make it extra special, I added a little watering can and a row of pink bobbles around the edge of the crown. The pleats are created by adding extra stitches and then pulling the carrying yarn very tightly behind the stitches being knitted. This is similar to the way old-fashioned tea cosies were created.

Size

To fit 2–4 years

Materials

1 x 50 g ball medium pink DK yarn
1 x 50 g ball bright green DK yarn
1 x 50 g ball sage green DK yarn
1 x 50 g ball bright pink DK yarn
Small amount pale pink DK yarn
Small amount variegated pink DK yarn
Small amount green cotton baby yarn

Pale green glass beads
Small piece cardboard
Polyester fiberfill
Size 6 (4 mm) double-pointed knitting needles
Size 3 (3.25 mm) double-pointed knitting needles
Size 1 (2.25 mm) knitting needles
Size C-2 (2.75 mm) crochet hook

Yarn needle
Beading needle
Sewing needle
Green sewing thread

Special Stitch

Mb (make bobble): (K1, p1, k1, p1, k1) in next st; turn, purl next 5 sts; turn, knit next 5 sts; turn, purl next 5 sts; turn. Sl1 knitwise, k2tog twice, psso.

Hat

Using size 6 double-pointed knitting needles and medium pink, cast on 90 sts. Join into a ring, being careful not to twist sts.

Work 12 rounds k1, p1 rib.

Increase round 1: Kfb in all sts (180 sts).

Increase round 2: *K1, kfb in next st; rep from * to end (270 sts).

Break off medium pink and join in bright green and bright pink.

Pleat round: *K9 green, k9 pink; repeat from * to end, pulling the yarn not in use very firmly across the back of the work. (This will cause the knitting to feel quite tight; this is correct. It will create the pleats.) Rep this round until work measures 5¹/₂ in. from beg of ribbing. Break off green.

Decrease round 1: *K2tog twice, k1, k2tog twice; rep from * to end (150 sts).

Decrease round 2: *K2tog, k1, k2tog; rep from * to end (90 sts).

Bobble setup rounds 1–3: With bright pink, knit.

Join pale pink.

Bobble round: *K4 with bright pink, mb with pale pink; rep from * to end of round.

Knit 2 rounds even with bright pink. Break off bright pink; join medium pink.

Crown shaping

Round 1: *K7, k2tog; rep from * to end (80 sts).

Round 2 and all even rounds: Knit.

Round 3: *K6, k2tog; rep from * to end (70 sts).

Round 5: *K5, k2tog; rep from * to end (60 sts).

Continue decreasing in this pattern until 20 sts remain. Break off yarn. Thread through rem sts, pull up tightly, and fasten off.

I-Cord Leaves

Using size 3 double-pointed knitting needles, and bright green, cast on 3 sts. Work an I-cord as follows: *Knit all sts. *Do not turn.* Switch right-hand needle to left hand and pull sts to other end of needle. Pull yarn firmly around behind work, ready to knit into the first st again. Repeat from * until I-cord stem measures 1 in. Now work forward and backward in rows, beginning the first row by switching the work to the left hand without turning and pulling the yarn around behind the work, as in the basic I-cord.

Row 1: Knit.

Row 2: Purl.

Row 3: K1, m1, k1 tbl, m1, k1.

Row 4 and all even rows: K1, purl to last st, k1.

Row 5: K2, m1, k1 tbl, m1, k2.

Row 7: K3, m1, k1 tbl, m1, k3.

Row 9: K4, m1, k1 tbl, m1, k4.

Row 11: K5, m1, k1 tbl, m1, k5.

Row 13: K5, sl2, k1, p2sso, k5.

Row 15: K4, sl2, k1, p2sso, k4.

Row 17: K3, sl2, k1, p2sso, k3.

Row 19: K2, sl2, k1, p2sso, k2.

Row 21: K1, sl2, k1, p2sso, k1.
Row 23: Sl2 sts, k1, p2sso.
Fasten off. Make 10 in all, 5 in bright green and 5 in sage green.

Watering Can

Using size 1 knitting needles and green baby yarn, cast on 45 sts.
Rows 1–3: Knit.
Row 4: Purl.
Row 5: Knit.
Row 6: Purl.
Row 7–27: Rep rows 5 and 6.
Rows 29–30: Knit
Row 31: Purl.
Row 32: Knit.
Row 33: Purl.

Base Shaping
Row 34: *K3, k2tog; rep from * to end (36 sts).

Row 35 and all odd rows: Purl.
Row 36: *K2, k2tog; rep from * to end (27 sts).
Row 38: *K1, k2tog; rep from * to end (18 sts).
Row 40: *K2tog; rep from * to end (9 sts).
Break off yarn, pull up tightly, and fasten off.
With right sides together, whipstitch edges together. Weave in ends. Turn right side out. Cut out a cardboard circle the same size as the base of the watering can and put in place.

Spout
With size 1 knitting needles and green baby yarn, cast on 8 sts.
Row 1: Knit.
Row 2: Purl.
Row 3: Kfb, knit to last 2 sts, kfb, k1.
Row 4: Purl.
Row 5: Knit.
Row 6: Purl.
Rows 7–18: Repeat rows 3–6.
Row 19: Ssk, knit to last 2 sts, k2tog.
Row 20: Purl.
Repeat rows 19–20 until 4 sts remain, ending with a row 19. Bind off on right side.
With right sides together and beginning at cast-on edge, whipstitch edges together until you reach the increase rows.
Turn right side out and stuff firmly. Sew the open end to the side of the watering can, 4 rows above the base of the can. Add more stuffing as needed.

Watering Can Rose
With size 1 knitting needles and green baby yarn, cast on 12 sts.
Row 1: Kfb in every st (24 sts).
Row 2: Purl.
Row 3: Knit.
Row 4: Purl.
Rows 5–6: Knit.
Rows 7–8: Purl.
Row 9: Knit.
Row 10: Purl.
Row 11: *K1, k2tog; rep from * to end. (16 sts)
Row 12: K2tog to end. (8 sts)
Break off yarn, pull up tightly, and fasten off.
With right sides together, whipstitch edges together. Turn right side out and stuff firmly. Sew securely to the end of the spout. Sew green glass beads to the rose.

Handles

With size 1 knitting needles and green baby yarn, cast on 3 sts. Work an I-cord as follows: *Knit all sts. *Do not turn.* Switch right-hand needle to left hand and pull sts to other end of needle. Pull yarn firmly around behind work, ready to knit into the first st again. Repeat from * until I-cord is desired length. Sl1, k2tog, psso; fasten off. Make one I-cord 2 1/2 in. long and one 5 in. long. Attach the 5 in. cord to the top of the watering can and the 2 1/2 in. cord to the back of the watering can to form handles.

Roses

With a size C-2 crochet hook, ch 48 loosely; turn.

Row 1: Tr in 4th ch from hook and in every ch across.

Row 2: Ch 3, dc into each tr to last 2 tr, sc in next tr, sl st in last tr.

Fasten off.

Starting at the end with the sl st, roll up the rose. Sew securely at the base.

Make 6 roses, 2 in medium pink, 2 in variegated pink, and 2 in pale pink.

Flowers for the Watering Can

With a size C-2 crochet hook and medium pink, ch 4; join into a ring with a sl st.

Round 1 (right side): Ch 2. Work 9 sc in center of ring, sl st in beginning ch-2. Break off medium pink.

Round 2: Join pale pink in sl st of rnd 1. Ch 3, 1 tr in each sc, sl st in beginning ch-3.

Fasten off.

Weave in ends and form into a neat circular shape.

Make 3.

Sew the flowers to the opening at the top of the watering can.

Finishing

Sew the watering can securely in the center of the crown. Sew the six cro-cheted roses around the watering can, then sew the stems of the leaves to the edge of the crown, along the bobble round.

The Tea Party

This hat is shaped like a cupcake with a little tea party on top—complete with a teapot, jam tarts, and cream pies. This is a very feminine beanie. The basic hat is very quick to knit, but take your time with the decorations and your patience will pay off.

Size
To fit 18 months to 2 years

Materials
1 x 50 g ball pink variegated DK yarn

1 x 50 g ball cream DK yarn

Small amounts of baby yarn in pale pink, bright blue, fawn, crimson, white, and cream

Stranded embroidery floss in pale blue

Polyester fiberfill

Cardboard scrap

Chenille pipe cleaner

Size 6 (4 mm) double-pointed knitting needles

Size 1 (2.25 mm) knitting needles

Size C-2 (2.75 mm) crochet hook

Sewing needle

Yarn needle

Hat

Using size 6 double-pointed knitting needles and variegated pink, cast on 90 sts. Join to work in round, being careful not to twist sts.
Work 34 rounds k1, p1 ribbing.
Break off pink and join cream.
Next round: Purl.
Next round: Knit.
Cont to knit every round until piece measures 7 1/2 in. from cast-on edge.

Crown Shaping

Round 1: *K7, k2tog; rep from * to end of round (80 sts).
Round 2: Knit.
Round 3: *K6, k2tog; rep from * to end of round (70 sts).
Round 4: Knit.

Round 5: *K5 k2tog; rep from * to end of round (60 sts).
Continue decreasing in this pattern until 10 sts remain.
Break off yarn, thread through rem sts, pull up tightly, and fasten off. Weave in all ends on wrong side.

Crochet Frill

With size C-2 crochet hook and cream, insert hook into a purl loop on the purl row at the top of the ribbed section.
*Ch 3, sc into next purl loop; rep from * around hat, finishing with a sl st in first st.

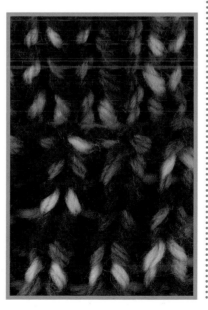

Teapot

Using size 1 knitting needles and bright blue baby yarn, cast on 9 sts.
Row 1: Purl.
Row 2: Kfb in each st (18 sts).
Row 3: Purl.
Join white.
Row 4: With white, knit.
Row 5: Purl.
Row 6: With blue, knit.
Row 7: Purl.
Rows 8–11: Rep rows 4–7.
Row 12: With white, knit.
Row 13: *P1, p2tog; rep from * to end. Break off white. (12 sts)
Rows 14–15: With blue, purl.
Row 16: Knit.
Row 17: P2tog to end (6 sts).
Row 18: Kfb in every st (12 sts).
Break off yarn, thread through rem sts, pull up tightly, and fasten off.

Cut a cardboard base the size of a small coin. With right sides together, sew edges to the halfway point, then insert the carboard coin in the base. Turn the teapot right side out and stuff firmly. To create a knob, use a spare strand of blue yarn and attach to top of teapot by weaving in on wrong side. Once secure, wrap remaining yarn tightly around top stitches (where decreases create a notch). Weave remaining yarn into work to secure. Continue stuffing the teapot until you have a firm round shape. Close seam.

Jam Tart
Jam Filling
Using size 1 knitting needles and crimson baby yarn, cast on 16 sts.

Row 1: Knit.

Row 2: P2tog to end.

Break off yarn, thread through rem sts, pull up tightly, and fasten off. Sew short ends together to form jam center. Weave in ends.

Make 2.

Pastry Casing
Using size 1 knitting needles and fawn baby yarn, cast on 24 sts. Bind off. Sew short ends together to form a ring.

Make 2.

Place jam center in pastry casing and sew into place.

Plate
Using size 1 knitting needles and bright blue baby yarn, cast on 35 sts.

Rows 1–3: Knit.

Row 4: *P1, p2tog; rep from * to end.

Row 5: Knit.

Row 6: P2tog to end.

Break off yarn, thread through rem sts, pull up tightly, and fasten off. Sew ends of rows together to form a circle. Weave in ends.

Sew a jam tart on each plate.

Spout
Using size 1 knitting needles and bright blue baby yarn, cast on 6 sts.

Row 1: Knit.

Row 2: Purl.

Row 3: Knit

Row 4: P2, p2tog, p2.

Rows 5–7: Repeat rows 1–3.

Bind off.

Fold spout in half. Cut pipe cleaner to fit, bending sharp ends over. Sew up side and wider end with pipe cleaner inside. Sew the smaller end of the spout to the teapot at the second blue stripe. Bend the spout into shape.

Handle
Using size 1 knitting needles and bright blue baby yarn, cast on 2 sts. Make an I-cord as follows: *Knit all sts. *Do not turn.* Switch right-hand needle to left hand and pull sts to other end of needle. Pull yarn firmly around behind work, ready to knit into the first st again. Rep from * until I-cord measures 1 1/4 in. Sl1, k1, psso; fasten off. Attach to teapot opposite spout.

Cream Pie

Pie Base

Using size 1 knitting needles and two strands of fawn baby yarn, cast on 24 sts.

Row 1: Break off one strand of yarn. Knit to end.

Row 2: Knit.

Row 3: *K1, k2tog; rep from * to end.

Row 4: Purl.

Row 5: K2tog to end.

Break off yarn, thread through rem sts, pull up tightly, and fasten off. Fold in half and sew edges together. Weave in ends and form into a circle.

Cream Top

Using size 1 knitting needles and cream baby yarn, cast on 16 sts.

Row 1: Purl.

Row 2: * K1, kfb; rep from * to end (24 sts).

Row 3: Purl.

Row 4: Knit.

Row 5: Purl.

Row 6: *K1, k2tog; rep from * to end (16 sts).

Row 7: P2tog to end.

Break off yarn, thread through rem sts, pull up tightly, and fasten off. Sew edges together and stuff with a little fiberfill to make a round shape. Sew onto pie base, enclosing fiberfill under cream top.

Make 2.

Flowers

Using size 1 knitting needles and pale pink baby yarn, cast on 16 sts.

Row 1: Knit.

Row 2: P2tog to end.

Break off yarn, thread through rem sts, pull up tightly, and fasten off. Fold in half and sew short ends together. Weave in ends and shape into a circle.

Using blue embroidery floss, work a couple of small straight stitches in the center of each flower and a bullion knot on top of the straight stitches. Make 10.

Finishing

Sew teapot securely to center of crown and then sew the jam tarts and the cream pies around the teapot. Sew the flowers at intervals around the hat.

Blackberry Pie

What better way to keep your head warm in winter than to have your own blackberry pie to wear? This whimsical beanie is complete with pie crust, ornamental knitted blackberries, and leaves. It's a great hat for a budding chef or keen gardener.

Size

To fit 2–4 years

Materials

1 x 50 g ball oatmeal DK yarn

2 x 50 g balls purple DK yarn

Small amount green DK yarn for leaves

Small amount of purple baby yarn for mini pie

Small amount of deep pink baby yarn for berries

Small amount of green baby yarn for calyxes

216 dark purple glass beads with big enough holes to thread onto baby yarn

Size 6 (4 mm) double-pointed knitting needles

Size 1 (2.25 mm) knitting needles

Size 2 (2.75 mm) double-pointed knitting needles

Size C-2 (2.75 mm) crochet hook

Yarn needle

Polyester fiberfill

Special Stitch

M5 (make 5): (p1, k1, p1, k1, p1) in same st, making 5 sts from one.

Mb (make bobble): (K1, p1, k1, p1, k1) in next st; turn, purl next 5 sts; turn, knit next 5 sts; turn, purl next 5 sts; turn. Sl1 knitwise, k2tog twice, psso.

Pb (place bead): Slide bead up yarn so that it sits directly next to right needle, k next st.

Hat

Using size 6 double-pointed knitting needles and oatmeal, cast on 90 sts. Join to work in round, being careful not to twist sts.

Work 30 rounds of k1, p1 rib. Break off oatmeal and join purple.

Next round: Purl, increasing 1 st (91 sts).

Begin blackberry stitch pattern (worked over 8 rows):

Round 1 and all odd rounds: Purl.

Round 2: P1, *m5, p1; rep from * to end.

Round 4: P1, *(sl1 purlwise) twice, k3tog, p2sso, k1; rep from * to end.

Round 6: P1, *p1, m5, p1; rep from * to end.

Round 8: P1, *p1, (sl1 purlwise) twice, k3tog, p1; rep from * to end.

Repeat these 8 rounds until work measures 7 in. from cast-on edge.

Decrease round: K2tog, k to end (90 sts).

Join oatmeal.

Bobble setup rounds 1 and 2: With oatmeal, knit.

Bobble round: *K4 with oatmeal, mb with purple; rep from * to end.

Break off purple and continue with oatmeal.

Knit 2 rounds even.

Crown Shaping

Round 1: *K7, k2tog; rep from * to end of round (80 sts).

Round 2: Knit.

Round 3: *K6, k2tog; rep from * to end of round (70 sts).

Round 4: Knit.

Round 5: *K5, k2tog; rep from * to end of round (60 sts).

Continue decreasing in this pattern until 10 sts remain.

Break off yarn, thread through rem sts, pull up tightly, and fasten off. Weave in all ends on wrong side.

Pie Crust

Crochet edging is worked into the purl bumps where ribbing and purple body of hat meet.

Using size C-2 crochet hook and oatmeal, insert hook into purple purl bump and work a sl st. *Ch 3, sc into next purl bump; rep from * around. Join with a sl st in first ch-3 loop. Fasten off and weave in ends.

Mini Pie

With size 1 knitting needles and two strands of oatmeal, cast on 24 sts. Break off one strand of yarn.

Row 1: Knit.

Row 2: Purl.

Row 3: *K1, k2tog; rep from * to end.

Row 4: Purl.

Row 5: K2tog; rep to end.

Break off yarn. Thread through rem sts, pull up tightly, and fasten off. Sew the edges together to make the base of the pie.

Filling

Using size 1 knitting needles and purple baby yarn, cast on 16 sts.
Row 1: Purl.
Row 2: *K1, kfb; rep from * to end (24 sts).
Row 3: Purl.
Row 4: Knit.
Row 5: Purl.
Row 6: *K1, k2tog; rep from * to end.
Row 7: P2tog; rep to end.
Break off yarn. Thread through rem sts, pull up tightly, and fasten off.

Finishing

Sew edges together. With the st st side facing out, place filling over base. Fill with a little polyester fibrerfill and stitch the filling down around the inside of the base to form a plump pie.

Blackberries

Thread 36 beads onto the purple baby yarn. Using size 1 double-pointed needles, cast on 3 sts.
Row 1: (wrong side) Pfb, p1, pfb (5 sts).
Row 2: (K1, pb) twice, k1.
Row 3: Pfb, p3, pfb (7 sts).
Rows 4, 6 and 8: (K1, pb) to last st, k1.
Row 5: Pfb, p5, pfb (9 sts).
Row 7: Pfb, p7, pfb (11 sts).
Row 9: K1, p9, k1.

Row 10: K2, (pb, k1) to last st, k1.
Row 11: Repeat row 9.
Row 12: (K1, pb) to last st, k1.
Row 13: Repeat row 9.
Row 14: Repeat row 10.
Row 15: Repeat row 9.
Row 16: Repeat row 12.
Row 17: Repeat row 9.
Row 18: Sl1, k1, psso, (pb, k1) to last 3 sts, pb, k2tog (9 sts).
Row 19: K1, p7, k1.
Bind off.
Make 6 (makes 3 berries).

Calyx

Using size 1 double-pointed needles and green baby yarn cast on 8 sts.
Row 1: (wrong side) Bind off 5 sts, k2 (3 sts).
Row 2: Cast on 5 sts (8 sts).
Repeat rows 1 and 2 four times. Bind off.

With right sides together, sew side seams of blackberry, leaving top open. Turn right side out. Stuff firmly with fiberfill, then sew top closed. Sew the calyx securely to the top of the blackberry.

Leaves

With size 2 double-pointed needles and green DK yarn, cast on 3 sts. Work an I-cord as follows: *Knit all sts. *Do not turn.* Switch right-hand needle to left hand and pull sts to other end of needle. Pull yarn firmly around behind work, ready to knit into the first st again. Repeat from *

until I-cord stem measures 1 in. Now work forward and backward in rows, beginning the first row by switching the work to the left hand without turning and pulling the yarn around behind the work, as in the basic I-cord.
Row 1: Knit.
Row 2: Purl.
Row 3: K1, m1, k1, m1, k1 (5 sts).
Row 4 and all even rows: K1, purl to last st, k1.
Row 5: K2, m1, k1, m1, k2 (7 sts).
Row 7: K3, m1, k1, m1, k3 (9 sts).
Row 9: K4, m1, k1, m1, k4 (11 sts).
Row 11: K5, m1, k1, m1, k5 (13 sts).
Row 13: K5, sl2, k1, p2sso (11 sts).
Row 15: K4, sl2, k1, p2sso (9 sts).
Row 17: K3, sl2, k1, p2sso (7 sts).
Row 19: K2, sl2, k1, p2sso (5 sts).
Row 21: K1, sl2, k1, p2sso (3 sts).
Row 22: Sl1, p2tog, psso (1 st). Fasten off.
Make 12.

Finishing

Sew three leaves radiating out from the center of the crown. Sew the pie to the top of the crown, surrounded by the three blackberries. Arrange the rest of the leaves evenly between the bobbles.

Autumn Harvest

With its autumnal color scheme, this fabulous headpiece is perfect for cooler days. Take your time when making the leaves and acorns, then set them aside to sew onto the finished hat. If you prefer a simpler style, knit just one or two different types of leaf. This project is ideal for using up all those odd remnants of wool.

Size
To fit 18 months to 2 years

Materials
1 x 50 g ball olive green DK yarn
1 x 50 g ball sage green DK yarn
1 x 50 g ball brown DK yarn
1 x 50 g ball beige DK yarn
1 x 50 g ball yellow-green DK yarn
1 x 50 g ball rust DK yarn

Size 2 (2.75 mm) double-pointed
    knitting needles
Size 5 (3.75 mm) double-pointed
    knitting needles
Size E-4 (3.5 mm) crochet hook
Yarn needle
Polyester fiberfill

Special Stitches

Mb (make bobble): (K1, p1, k1, p1, k1) in next st; turn, purl next 5 sts; turn, knit next 5 sts; turn, purl next 5 sts; turn. Sl1 knitwise, k2tog twice, psso.

Hat

Using size 5 double-pointed knitting needles and olive green, cast on 90 sts. Join to work in round, being careful not to twist sts.

Rounds 1–10: Knit.
Break off green; join brown and rust.
Rounds 11–21: *K1 with rust, p1 with brown; rep from * to end.
Break off rust, continuing in brown.
Round 22: Knit.
Round 23: Purl.
Break off brown; join sage green.
Round 24: Knit.
Round 25: Purl.
Join olive green.
Rounds 26–27: *K3 with olive, k3 with sage; rep from * to end.
Rounds 28–29: *K3 with sage, k3 with olive; rep from * to end.
Rounds 30–31: Repeat rounds 26–27.
Break off olive and continue in sage.
Round 32: Knit.
Round 33: Purl.
Break off sage and join brown.
Round 34: Knit.
Round 35: Purl.
Break off brown; join rust.
Rounds 36–37: Knit.
Join brown and beige (do not break off rust).

Round 38: *K2 with rust, mb with brown, k2 with rust, mb with beige; rep from * to end.
Break off brown and beige and continue in rust.
Rounds 39–41: Knit.
Break off rust and join brown.
Round 42: Knit.
Round 43: Purl.
Rounds 44–45: Knit.
Break off brown; join rust.
Rounds 46–47: Knit.
Break off rust; join beige.
Rounds 48–49: Knit.
Break off beige; join brown.

Round 50: Knit.
Round 51: Purl.
Break off brown; join beige.

Crown Shaping

Round 52: *K7, k2tog; rep from * to end (80 sts).
Round 53 and all odd rounds: Knit.
Round 54: *K6, k2tog; rep from * to end (70 sts).
Round 56: *K5, k2tog; rep from * to end (60 sts).
Continue decreasing in this pattern until 20 sts remain. Break off yarn. Thread through rem sts, pull up tightly, and fasten off.

Acorn

Using size 2 double-pointed knitting needles and brown, cast on 6 sts.
Row 1: (right side) Kfb in each st (12 sts).
Row 2: Kfb in each st (24 sts).
Row 3: *K1, p1; rep from * to end.
Row 4: *P1, k1; rep from * to end.
Rows 5–8: Repeat rows 3–4.
Row 9: *P1, p2tog; rep from * to end.
Break off brown and join beige.
Row 10: Purl.
Row 11: Knit.
Row 12–15: Repeat rows 10–11.
Row 16: Purl.
Row 17: *K2tog, k2; rep from * to end.
Row 18: Purl.
Row 19: *K2tog, k1; rep from * to end.
Row 20: P2tog to end.
Break off yarn, thread through rem sts, pull up tightly, and fasten off.

With brown, cast on 10 sts for the stem. Bind off.

Sew the stem to the cast on edge of the acorn. With right side out, seam acorn using ladder stitch, filling firmly with fiberfill as you go. Make 2.

Beech Leaf

With size 1 double-pointed needles, cast on 2 sts. Work an I-cord as follows: *Knit all sts. *Do not turn.* Switch right-hand needle to left hand and pull sts to other end of needle. Pull yarn firmly around behind work,

ready to knit into the first st again. Repeat from * until I-cord stem measures 1 in.
Now work forward and backward in rows, beginning the first row by switching the work to the left hand without turning and pulling the yarn around behind the work, as in the basic I-cord.
Row 1: Kfb, k1 (3 sts).
Row 2: Purl.
Row 3: K1, (yo, k1) twice (5 sts).
Row 4: P1, (k1, p1) twice.
Row 5: K1, p1, yo, k1, yo, p1, k1 (7 sts).
Row 6: P1, k1, p3, k1, p1.

Row 7: K1, p1, k1, yo, k1, yo, k1, p1, k1 (9 sts).
Row 8: *P1, k1; rep from * to last st, p1.
Row 9: (K1, p1) twice, yo, k1, yo, (p1, k1) twice (11 sts).
Row 10: (P1, k1) twice, p3, (k1, p1) twice.
Row 11: (K1, p1) twice, k1, yo, k1, yo, k1, (p1, k1) twice (13 sts).
Row 12: *P1, k1; rep from * to last st, p1.
Row 13: *K1, p1; rep from * to last st, k1.
Row 14: Repeat row 12.
Row 15: Ssk, (k1, p1) 4 times, k1, k2tog (11 sts).
Row 16: Repeat row 13.
Row 17: Ssk, (p1, k1) 3 times, p1, k2tog (9 sts).
Row 18: Repeat row 12.
Row 19: Ssk, (K1, p1) twice, k1, k2tog (7 sts).
Row 20: Repeat row 13.
Row 21: Ssk, p1, k1, p1, k2tog (5 sts).
Row 22: Repeat row 12.
Row 23: Ssk, k1, k2tog (3 sts).
Row 24: Sl1, p2tog, psso (1 st). Fasten off.

Whitebeam Leaf

With size 1 double-pointed needles, cast on 2 sts. Work an I-cord as follows: *Knit all sts. *Do not turn.* Switch right-hand needle to left hand and pull sts to other end of needle. Pull yarn firmly around behind work, ready to knit into the first st again. Repeat from * until I-cord stem measures 1 in.

Now work forward and backward in rows, beginning the first row by switching the work to the left hand without turning and pulling the yarn around behind the work, as in the basic I-cord.

Row 1: Kfb, k1 (3 sts).
Row 2: Purl.
Row 3: K1, m1, k1, m1, k1 (5 sts).
Row 4 and all even rows: K1, purl to last st, k1.
Row 5: K2, m1, k1, m1, k2 (7 sts).
Row 7: K3, m1, k1, m1, k3 (9 sts).
Row 9: K4, m1, k1, m1, k4 (11 sts).
Row 11: K5, m1, k1, m1, k5 (13 sts).
Row 13: K5, sl2, k1, p2sso (11 sts).
Row 15: K4, sl2, k1, p2sso (9 sts).
Row 17: K3, sl2, k1, p2sso (7 sts).
Row 19: K2, sl2, k1, p2sso (5 sts).
Row 21: K1, sl2, k1, p2sso (3 sts).
Row 22: Sl1, p2tog, psso (1 st). Fasten off.

Maple Leaf

With size 1 double-pointed knitting needles, cast on 11 sts.
Row 1: K2, m1, k3, sl1, k3, m1, k2 (13 sts).
Row 2 and all even rows (except when stated otherwise): Knit to center st, purl, knit to end.
Row 3: K2, m1, k4, sl1, k4, m1, k2 (15 sts).
Row 5: K2, m1, k5, sl1, k5, m1, k2 (17 sts).
Row 7: K2, m1, k6, sl1, k6, m1, k2 (19 sts).
Row 9: K2, m1, k7, sl1, k7, m1, k2 (21 sts).

Row 11: K2, m1, k8, sl1, k8, m1, k2 (23 sts).
Row 13: Bind off 6 sts, k5, sl1, k11 (17 sts).
Row 14: Bind off 6 sts, k5, p1, k5 (11 sts).
Rows 15–22: Repeat rows 1–8.
Row 23: Bind off 4 sts, k5, sl1, k9 (15 sts).
Row 24: Bind off 4 sts, k5, p1, k5 (11 sts).
Row 25: K1, ssk, k2, sl1, k2, k2tog, k1 (9 sts).
Row 27: K1, ssk, k1, sl1, k1, k2tog, k1 (7 sts).
Row 29: K1, ssk, sl1, k2tog, k1 (5 sts).
Row 31: Ssk, sl1, k2tog (3 sts).
Row 33: Sl1, k2tog, psso (1 st). Fasten off.

To make the stem, cast on 2 sts and make an I-cord (see instructions in other leaves) measuring 1 in. Fasten off. Attach to base of leaf.

Oak Leaf

Center vein: With size E-4 crochet hook, ch 12. Sl st in second ch from hook and in each ch across.
Stem: Ch 7. Sl st in second ch from hook and in each ch across. Join to base of center vein with a sl st.
Round 1: Working along back of center vein, sl st in next 2 sts; ch 7, sk first 3 chs, dc in next 2 chs, sc in next 2 chs (first lobe formed); sl st in next st of center vein, sc in next 3 sts, sl st in next st; ch 6, sk first 3 chs, dc in next 2 chs, sc in next ch (second lobe formed); sl st in next st of center vein, sc in next 3 sts; in turning ch, work 5 sc. Now working along top of center

vein, sc in next 3 sts, sl st in next st; ch 6, sk first 3 chs, dc in next 2 chs, sc in next ch; sl st in next st of center vein, sc in next 3 sts, sl st in next st; ch 7, sk first 3 chs, dc in next 2 chs, sc in next 2 chs; sl in next 2 sts of center vein. Fasten off.
Round 2: Join contrasting color at base of leaf. Sc in first sl st, sk next sl st; working along bottom of first lobe, sc in next 4 sts; in ch-3 at end of lobe, work 1 sc in first ch, 2 sc in next ch, 1 sc in next ch; sc in next 4 sts; sk next sl st, sc in next 3 sts, sk next sl st; working along bottom of second lobe, sc in next 3 sts; in ch-3, work 1 sc in first ch, 2 sc in next ch, 1 sc in next ch; sc in next 3 sts; sk next sl st, sc in next 3 sts; in 5 sc at end of leaf, work 1 sc in first st, 2 sc in next 3 sts, 1 sc in last st. Work second side of leaf to match first side: Sc in next 3 sts, sk next sl st; sc in in next 3 sts along bottom of lobe; in ch-3 work 1 sc, 2 sc, 1 sc; sc in next 3 sts; sk next sl st, sc in next 3 sts, sk next sl st; sc in next 4 sts along bottom of lobe; in ch-3 work 1 sc, 2 sc, 1 sc; sc in next 4 sts; sk next sl st, sc in last sl st. Sl st in each st along bottom edge of stem; in turning ch work 3 sl st, sl st in each st along top edge of stem; join with sl st in beginning sc. Fasten off.

Finishing

Make an assortment of leaves in your choice of colors and styles from the patterns given above. Arrange leaves and acorns on and around the crown of the hat and sew securely in place.

Ho, Ho, Ho

Perfect for a stocking filler, this bright and colourful Christmas hat sets the tone perfectly, with cream holly leaves and red berries emanating from a central bobble on the crown. A soft mohair brim and snuggly wool are sure to make this hat a hit.

Sizes

To fit 12–18 months (instructions for 2 to 3 years in parentheses)

Materials

1 x 50 g ball cream mohair DK yarn
1 x 50 g ball red DK yarn
Size 6 (4 mm) double-pointed
    knitting needles
Size 1 (2.25 mm) double-pointed
    knitting needles

Size C-2 (2.75 mm) crochet hook
Yarn needle
Polyester fiberfill

Special Stitch

W&t (wrap and turn) [knit side]: Slip next stitch purlwise to right needle, then bring yarn to the front. Slip the same stitch back to the left needle, then return yarn to the back and turn the work.

W&t (wrap and turn) [purl side]: Slip next stitch purlwise to right needle, then bring yarn to the back. Slip the same stitch back to the left needle, then return yarn to the front and turn the work.

Hat

Using size 6 double-pointed knitting needles and cream mohair, cast on 92 (102) sts. Join to work in round, being careful not to twist stitches.
Rounds 1–10: Knit.
Break off mohair and join red.
Work in k2, p2 rib for 12 (14) rounds.
Next round: Knit, decreasing 2 sts.
Knit even until hat measures 6 (6 1/2) in. from rolled brim.

Crown Shaping

Round 1: *K7 (8), k2tog; rep from * to end of round (80 [90] sts).
Round 2: Knit.
Round 3: *K6 (7), k2tog; rep from * to end of round (70 [80] sts).
Round 4: Knit.
Round 5: *K5 (6), k2tog; rep from * to end of round (60 [70] sts).
Continue decreasing in this pattern until 10 sts remain.
Break off yarn, thread through rem sts, pull up tightly, and fasten off. Weave in all ends on wrong side.

Knitted Ball

Using size 1 knitting needles and cream mohair, cast on 12 sts.
Row 1: Knit.
Row 2: P10, w&t.
Row 3: K8, w&t.
Row 4: P6, w&t.
Row 5: K4, w&t.
Row 6: Purl.
Repeat these 6 rows 4 times. Bind off. With right sides together, sew side seam halfway. Turn right side out and stuff firmly with fiberfill. Sew the remainder of the seam and then run a gathering thread around the top edge. Pull up firmly and fasten off. Do the same with the other end. Make one.

Holly Leaves

Round 1: With size C-2 crochet hook, ch 12 loosely. Starting in the second ch from hook, *sc in next ch, hdc in next ch, dc in next ch, 2 dc in next ch, 2 tr in next ch, 1 tr in next ch, 2 tr in next ch, 2 dc in next ch, dc in next ch, hdc in next ch, sc in next ch.** Ch 3, sl st in second ch from hook, sc in next ch. Working along other side of foundation ch, rep from *, ending at **. Do not break yarn.

Stem and edging: Ch 9, sl st into 2nd ch from hook and in each ch across. Continue along sts of round 1 as follows: sc in next 2 sts; *ch 3, sl st in second ch from hook, sc in next ch; sc in next 3 sts; (ch 4, sl st in second ch from hook, sc in next ch, hdc in next chain, sk next st, sc in next 3 sts) twice; ch 3, sl st in second ch from hook, sc in next ch**; sc in next st, sl st in next 8 sts (around point of leaf), sc in next st; rep from *, ending at **; sc in next 2 sts; join with sl st to base of stem. Fasten off.
Make 5.

Holly Berries

Using size 1 double-pointed knitting needles and red, cast on 1 st.
Row 1: K1, p1, k1, p1, k1 into same st (5 sts).
Row 2: Knit.
Row 3: Purl.
Row 4: Knit, do not turn. *Sl second st over first; rep from * until 1 st rem. Fasten off.

Run a gathering thread around the outside of the bobble. Gather tightly to form a round bobble.
Make 2 berries for each holly leaf and attach them to the tops of the leaves.

Finishing

Sew the ends of the holly stems to the top of the crown. Sew the knitted ball on top.

Fin's Penguin

My young grandson Fin loves all things penguin, and I have already made him many penguin items. The body and head of this penguin are knitted in the round so he has a beautiful seamless shape. His wings, feet, and scarf are knitted on two needles. Some patience is required as the pieces are small, but the results are worth the effort.

Size
To fit 18 months to 2 years

Materials
1 x 50 g ball cream mohair DK yarn
1 x 50 g ball red DK yarn
1 x 50 g ball black DK yarn
Small amounts of baby yarn in red, black, white, and orange
Size 6 (4 mm) double-pointed knitting needles
Size 1 (2.25 mm) double-pointed knitting needles
Polyester fiberfill
Yarn needle

Special Stitch

Mb (make bobble): (K1, p1, k1, p1, k1) in next st; turn, purl next 5 sts; turn, knit next 5 sts; turn, purl next 5 sts; turn. Sl1 knitwise, k2tog twice, psso.

Hat

Using size 6 double-pointed knitting needles and cream mohair, cast on 95 sts.

Round 1: Knit.

Round 2: K2, *mb, k5; rep from * to last 2 sts, k2.

Round 3: Knit, decreasing 3 sts evenly (92 sts).

Break off cream and join red and black DK yarn.

Round 4–15: *K2 red, p2 black; rep from * to end.

Break off red.

Round 16: Knit.

Round 17: Purl.

Round 18: Knit.

Break off black; join cream mohair.

Round 19: Knit.

Round 20: K1, *mb, k4; rep from * to last st, k1.

Rounds 21–22: Knit.

Break off cream and join black.

Rounds 23–25: Repeat rounds 16–18.

Break off black and join cream.

Round 26: Knit.

Round 27: K2, *mb, k4; rep from * end.

Rounds 28–29: Knit.

Break off cream and join black.

Rounds 30–32: Repeat rounds 16–18.

Break off black and join cream.

Rounds 33–43: Repeat rounds 19–29.

Break off cream; join black and red.

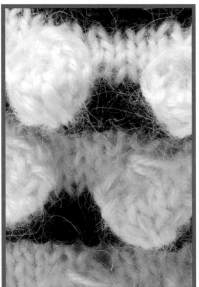

Crown Shaping

Work in alternate roounds of red and black.

Round 1: *K7, k2tog; rep from * to end of round (80 sts).

Round 2: Knit.

Round 3: *K6, k2tog; rep from * to end of round (70 sts).

Round 4: Knit.

Round 5: *K5, k2tog; rep from * to end of round (60 sts).

Continue decreasing in this pattern until 10 sts remain.

Break off yarn, thread through rem sts, pull up tightly, and fasten off. Weave in ends.

Penguin

Head

Using size 1 double-pointed knitting needles and black baby yarn, cast on 9 sts. Join to work in round, being careful not to twist the sts.

Round 1: Knit.
Round 2: *K1, m1, k1, m1, k1; rep from * to end of round (15 sts).
Rounds 3–6: Knit.
Round 7: *Ssk, k2tog; rep from * to end of round (9 sts).
Round 8: Knit.
Stuff head with polyester fiberfill. Break off yarn, thread through rem sts, pull up tightly, and fasten off.

Body

With black, repeat first 3 rounds of head.
Round 4: *K1, m1, k3, m1, k1; rep from * to end of round.
Rounds 5–11: Knit.

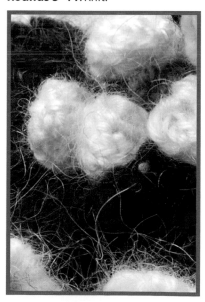

Round 12: *Ssk, k3, k2tog; rep from * to end of round.
Round 13: Knit.
Round 14: *Ssk, k2tog; rep from * to end of round (9 sts).
Round 15: Knit.
Stuff body with fiberfill. Break off yarn, thread through rem sts, pull up tightly, and fasten off.

Tummy

Using size 1 needles and white baby yarn, cast on 3 sts.
Row 1: Purl.
Row 2: Kfb, k1, kfb (5 sts).
Row 3: Purl.
Row 4: Knit.
Row 5–19: Repeat rows 3–4, ending with a purl row.
Row 20: Ssk, k1, k2tog.
Row 21: Purl.
Row 22: Sl1, k2tog, psso.
Fasten off.

Center the tummy panel on the front of the body and sew in place with very small stitches.

Face

Using size 1 needles and white baby yarn, cast on 1 st.
Row 1: Knit.
Row 2: Knit in front loop of stitch, then back loop, then front loop again (3 sts).
Row 3: Purl.
Row 4: Kfb, k1, kfb (5 sts).
Row 5: Purl. Bind off purlwise.
Sew onto the head with the point facing down. Attach the head securely to the top of the body, aligning the face with the top of the tummy piece.

Wings

Using size 1 needles and black baby yarn, cast on 3 sts.
Row 1: Purl.
Row 2: Kfb, k1, kfb (5 sts).
Row 3: Purl.
Row 4: Knit.
Row 5–13: Repeat rows 3–4, ending with a purl row.
Row 14: Ssk, k1, k2tog.
Row 15: Purl.
Row 16: Sl1, k2tog, psso.
Fasten off.
Make 2. Attach a wing to the neckline at each side of the body.

Beak

Using size 1 needles and orange baby yarn, cast on 3 sts.

Rows 1–3: Knit.

Bind off.

Roll up very tightly into a tube and sew closed. Attach to the center of the face.

Eyes

With 3 strands of black embroidery thread, work a bullion knot for each eye. Tie off under the neckline.

Feet

Using size 1 needles and orange baby yarn, cast on 9 sts.

Row 1: Purl.

Row 2: Ssk, knit to last 2 sts, k2tog. (7 sts)

Row 3: P2tog, purl to last 2 sts, p2tog tbl. (5 sts)

Row 4: Repeat row 2. (3 sts)

Row 5: Purl.

Row 6: K1, m1, knit to last st, m1, k1. (5 sts)

Row 7: Kfb, purl to last st, kfb. (7 sts)

Row 8: Repeat row 6. (9 sts)

Bind off all sts.

With right sides together, sew cast-on edge to bind-off edge. Turn right side out and sew open edges together. Attach to underside of penguin with sewn edges facing forward.

Scarf

Using size 1 needles and red baby yarn, cast on 3 sts.

Work in garter st (every row knit), until scarf measures 4 in. Bind off.

Tie in a knot around the penguin's neck.

Snowballs

Using size 1 needles and cream mohair, cast on 1 st. Work a bobble. Break off yarn and fasten off. Make as many as you like.

Finishing

Attach penguin to crown of hat.

Sew snowballs around the penguin's feet.

Frog in a Pond

Any frog fan will be delighted with this tiny creature sitting atop his leaves in the center of the pond. This hat is a good challenge for an advancing knitter. Take the time to make your frog carefully, as it will be the focus of attention.

Size

To fit 18 months to 2 years

Materials

1 x 50 g ball yellow-green DK yarn
1 x 50 g ball olive green DK yarn
1 x 50 g ball light blue DK yarn
1 x 50 g ball bright blue variegated DK yarn
1 x 50 g ball light green cotton baby yarn

Black stranded embroidery floss
Size 5 (3.75 mm) double-pointed knitting needles
Size 1 (2.25 mm) double-pointed knitting needles
Polyester fiberfill
Yarn needle

Special Stitch

Mb (make bobble): (K1, p1, k1, p1, k1) in next st; turn, purl next 5 sts; turn, knit next 5 sts; turn, purl next 5 sts; turn. Sl1 knitwise, k2tog twice, psso.

Gauge

24 sts in stockinette st on size 5 needles = 4 in.

Hat

Using size 5 double-pointed knitting needles and yellow-green, cast on 92 sts. Join to work in round.
Rounds 1–10: Knit.
Join light blue.
Rounds 11–23: *K2 with light blue, p2 with yellow-green; rep from * to end.
Break off light blue.
Round 24: Knit, decreasing 2 sts evenly.

Round 25: Purl.
Break off yellow-green; join olive green.
Round 26: Knit.
Round 27: Purl.
Break off olive, join light blue.
Rounds 28–29: Repeat rounds 26–27.
Join bright blue.
Rounds 30–31: With bright blue, repeat rounds 26–27.
Rounds 32–33: With light blue, knit.
Round 34: *K4 with light blue, mb with bright blue; rep from * to end.
Rounds 35–36: Repeat rounds 32–33.
Break off light blue and continue in bright blue.
Rounds 37–38: Repeat rounds 26–27.
Break off bright blue; join yellow-green and olive.
Round 39: With olive, knit.

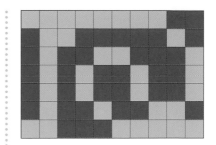

Rounds 40–46: Follow the color-work chart (repeating the 10 sts of the chart nine times over each round).
Join bright blue.
Rounds 47–48: With bright blue, repeat rounds 26–27.
Break off bright blue; join light blue.
Rounds 49–50: With light blue, repeat rounds 26–27.
Rounds 51–52: With olive, repeat rounds 26–27.
Rounds 53–54: With yellow-green, repeat rounds 26–27.

Break off olive and yellow-green and continue in light blue for the remainder of the hat.

Crown Shaping
Round 55: *K7, k2tog; rep from * to end (80 sts).
Round 56 and all even rounds: Knit.
Round 57: *K6, k2tog; rep from * to end (70 sts).
Round 59: *K5, k2tog; rep from * to end (60 sts).
Continue decreasing in this pattern until 20 sts remain. Break off yarn. Thread through rem sts, pull up tightly, and fasten off.
Weave in all ends.

Frog
Head
Using size 1 double-pointed knitting needles and green baby yarn, cast on 9 sts. Join to work in round, being careful not to twist the sts.
Round 1: Knit.
Round 2: *K1, m1; rep from * to end of round (15 sts).
Rounds 3–6: Knit.
Round 7: *Ssk, k1, k2tog; rep from * to end (9 sts).
Round 8: Knit.
Leave sts on needle and stuff head firmly to make a round shape; then thread yarn through rem sts, pull up tightly, and fasten off.

Eyes, Feet, and Hands
These are all made as bobbles and then sewn onto the head and the ends of the arms and legs.
Using size 1 double-pointed knitting needles and green baby yarn, cast on 1 st.
Row 1: Knit into the front, back and front again (3 sts).
Row 2: Knit.
Row 3: Purl.
Row 4: Knit. Do not turn work. Pass 2nd, 3rd, and 4th sts one at a time over the first st. Fasten off. Work running stitch around the outside and pull up to form a bobble.
Make 6.

Body
Using size 1 double-pointed knitting needles and green baby yarn, cast on 9 sts. Join to work in round, being careful not to twist the sts.
Round 1: Knit.
Round 2: *K1, m1; rep from * to end of round (15 sts).
Rounds 3–7: Knit.
Round 8: *K1, m1, k3, m1, k1; rep from * to end (21 sts).
Rounds 9–12: Knit.
Round 13: *Ssk, k3, k2tog; rep from * to end (15 sts).
Round 14: Knit.
Round 15: *Ssk, k1, k2tog; rep from * to end (9sts).
Round 16: Knit.
Leave sts on needle and stuff body firmly to make a round shape. Then thread yarn through rem sts, pull up tightly, and fasten off.

Legs and Arms

Using size 1 double-pointed knitting needles and green baby yarn, cast on 2 sts. Make an I-cord as follows: *Knit all sts. *Do not turn.* Switch right-hand needle to left hand and pull sts to other end of needle. Pull yarn firmly around behind work, ready to knit into the first st again. Repeat from * until I-cord measures 1 in. Sl1, k2tog, psso, fasten off.
Make 4.

Finishing

Sew head securely to body. Sew arms to shoulders and sew legs at each side of body. Sew a bobble to the end of each arm and leg.
Sew the eyes to the top of the head, as shown in the photos. Work a French knot in black embroidery floss in the center of each eye. Give your frog a lovely big smile by mak-

ing a wide stitch across the middle of his face and anchoring it with a tiny stitch in the center. Fasten off under the body of the frog.

Leaves

With size 1 double-pointed needles, cast on 2 sts. Work an I-cord as follows: *Knit all sts. *Do not turn.* Switch right-hand needle to left hand and pull sts to other end of needle. Pull yarn firmly around behind work, ready to knit into the first st again. Repeat from * until I-cord stem measures 1 in.
Now work forward and backward in rows, beginning the first row by switching the work to the left hand without turning and pulling the yarn around behind the work, as in the basic I-cord.
Row 1: Kfb, k1 (3 sts).
Row 2: Purl.
Row 3: K1, m1, k1, m1, k1 (5 sts).
Row 4 and all even rows: K1, purl to last st, k1.
Row 5: K2, m1, k1, m1, k2 (7 sts).
Row 7: K3, m1, k1, m1, k3 (9 sts).
Row 9: K4, m1, k1, m1, k4 (11 sts).
Row 11: K5, m1, k1, m1, k5 (13 sts).
Row 13: K5, sl2, k1, p2sso (11 sts).
Row 15: K4, sl2, k1, p2sso (9 sts).
Row 17: K3, sl2, k1, p2sso (7 sts).
Row 19: K2, sl2, k1, p2sso (5 sts).
Row 21: K1, sl2, k1, p2sso (3 sts).
Row 22: Sl1, p2tog, psso (1 st). Fasten off.
Make 6 in olive green and 7 in yellow-green.

Finishing

Attach 12 leaves around to the top of the hat. Sew the frog to the center of the remaining leaf and then sew this leaf to the center of the crown.

Hop To It

Fans of rabbits will be delighted with this beanie, which features a plump white bunny clutching a juicy carrot in his tiny paw. Take your time making all the little pieces and you will end up with a fantastic result.

Sizes

To fit 18 months to 2 years (instructions for 3 to 4 years in parentheses)

Materials

1 x 50 g ball bright green DK yarn
Small amounts of brown, orange, and various shades of green DK yarn
Small amounts of white and orange cotton baby yarn
Stranded embroidery floss in black and pink
Polyester fiberfill

Size 6 (4 mm) double-pointed knitting needles
Size 1 (2.25 mm) double-pointed knitting needles
Size 2 (2.75 mm) double-pointed knitting needles
Yarn needle
Embroidery needle

Hat

Using size 6 double-pointed knitting needles and brown, cast on 90 (100) sts on 3 needles. Join to work in round, being careful not to twist the stitches.

Rounds 1–10: Knit.
Break off brown and join bright green.
Rounds 11–23 (25): *K1, p1; rep from * to end.
Rounds 24–25 (26–27): Knit.
Join orange.

Carrot motif

There will be 9 carrots on small hat, and 10 carrots on large hat.
Round 1: K2 green, *k1 orange, k9 green; rep from *, ending with k7 green.
Round 2: Repeat round 1.

Round 3: K2 green, *k2 orange, k8 green; rep from *, ending with k6 green.
Round 4: Repeat round 3.
Round 5: K2 green, *k3 orange, k7 green; rep from *, ending with k5 green.
Round 6: Repeat round 5.
Round 7: K3 green, *k3 orange, k7 green; rep from *, ending with k4 green.
Round 8: Repeat round 7.
Round 9: K3 green, *k4 orange, k6 green; rep from *, ending with k3 green.
Round 10: K4 green, *k3 orange, k7 green; rep from *, ending with k3 green.
Round 11: Repeat round 10. Join dark green.
Round 12: K4 bright green, *k3 orange, k3 dark green, k4 bright green; rep from *, ending with k2 green.
Round 13: K5 bright green, *k2 orange, k5 dark green, k3 bright green; rep from *, ending with k2 green. Break off orange and dark green.
Rounds 14–15: With bright green, knit.

Crown

Break off bright green and join brown.
Round 1: Knit.
Round 2: Purl.
Round 3: Knit.
Round 4: Purl.
Break off brown and join orange.
Round 5: Knit.
Round 6: Purl.

Round 7: *K7 (8), k2tog; rep from * to end (80 [90] sts).
Round 8: Purl.
Break off orange. Join in bright green and dark green and work the remainder of the crown in alternating rounds of the two colors.

Work in alternating rounds of bright green and mid green.
Round 9: *K6 (7), k2tog; rep from * to end of round (70 [80] sts).
Round 10: Knit.
Round 11: *K5 (6), k2tog; rep from * to end of round (60 [70] sts).
Round 12: Knit.
Round 13: *K4 (5), k2tog; rep from * to end of round (50 [60] sts).
Continue decreasing in this pattern until 10 sts remain.
Break off yarn, thread through rem sts, pull up tightly, and fasten off. Weave in all ends on wrong side.

Rabbit

Head

Using size 1 double-pointed knitting needles and white baby yarn, cast on 9 sts. Join to work in round.

Round 1: Knit.

Round 2: *K1, m1, k1, m1, k1; rep from * to end (15 sts).

Round 3: Knit.

Round 4: *K1, m1, k3, m1, k1; rep from * to end (21 sts).

Rounds 5–8: Knit.

Round 9: *K1, ssk, k1, k2tog, k1; rep from * to end (15 sts).

Rounds 10–11: Knit.

Round 12: *Ssk, k1, k2tog; rep from * to end (9 sts).

Round 13: Knit.

Leaving sts on needle, stuff head firmly. Run thread through rem sts, pull up tightly, and fasten off.

Body

Using size 1 double-pointed needles and white baby yarn, cast on 9 sts. Join to work in round.

Round 1–5: Work rounds 1–5 of head.

Round 6: *K1, m1, k5, m1, k1; rep from * to end (27 sts).

Rounds 7–15: Knit.

Round 16: *Ssk, k5, k2tog; rep from * to end (21 sts).

Round 17: Knit.

Round 18: *Ssk, k3, k2tog; rep from * to end (15 sts).

Round 19: Knit.

Round 20: *Ssk, k1, k2tog; rep from * to end (9 sts).

Round 21: Knit.

Leaving sts on needle, stuff body firmly. Run thread through rem sts, pull up tightly, and fasten off.

Ears

Using size 1 double-pointed needles and white baby yarn, cast on 2 sts. Work backwards and forwards in rows.

Row 1: Purl.

Row 2: K1, m1, k1.

Row 3: Purl.

Row 4: K1, m1, k1, m1, k1.

Row 5: Purl.

Row 6: Knit.

Row 7–19: Repeat rows 5–6, ending with a purl row.

Row 20: Ssk, k1, k2tog.

Row 21: Purl.

Bind off. Make 2.

I-Cord Legs and Arms

Using size 1 double-pointed needles and white baby yarn, cast on 3 sts. Make an I-cord as follows: *Knit all sts. *Do not turn.* Switch right-hand needle to left hand and pull sts to other end of needle. Pull yarn firmly around behind work, ready to knit into the first st again. Repeat from * until I-cord is the desired length. Sl1, k2tog, psso; fasten off.

Make two I-cords 1 1/2 in. long for the arms. Make two I-cords 2 in. long for the legs.

Feet, Paws, and Tail

These are made like a bobble and then stitched to the end of the legs and arms. Make 5 in all.

Using size 1 double-pointed needles and white baby yarn, cast on 1 st.

Row 1: K1, p1, k1, p1, k1 into the same stitch (5 sts).

Row 2: Purl.
Row 3: Knit.
Row 4: Purl.
Row 5: Knit. Do not turn. Slip the second stitch over the first on the right-hand needle. Repeat until 1 st remains. Fasten off.
Run a gathering stitch around the outside edge, draw up, and fasten off.
Make 5. Attach one to each arm and leg and keep one for the tail.

Scarf

Using size 1 double-pointed needles and orange baby yarn, cast on 3 sts. Work in k1, p1 rib for 4 in. Bind off. Weave in ends.

Carrot

Using size 1 double-pointed needles and orange baby yarn, cast on 1 st.
Row 1: Knit.
Row 2: Kfb.
Row 3: Knit.
Row 4: K1, m1, k1.
Row 5: Knit.
Row 6: K1, kfb, k1.
Row 7: Knit.
Row 8: K2, m1, k2.
Row 9: Knit.
Row 10: K2, kfb, k2.
Row 11: Knit.
Bind off.
Cut a couple of short pieces of green yarn for the carrot top. Roll up the carrot. Sew the side seam, enclosing the carrot tops in place as you go.

Finishing

Using 3 strands of black embroidery floss, make French knots for eyes on each side of the head. Use pink to embroider the nose. Tie off the threads where the head will attach to the body. Pin the ears on the back of the head and sew securely in place.
Sew the head to the body, then sew the arms to each side of the body. Sew the carrot firmly to one paw. Sew the legs to the body at the hips. Dress the rabbit with the scarf.

Leaves

With size 2 double-pointed needles, cast on 3 sts. Work an I-cord as follows: *Knit all sts. *Do not turn.* Switch right-hand needle to left hand and pull sts to other end of needle. Pull yarn firmly around behind work, ready to knit into the first st again. Repeat from * until I-cord stem measures 1 in.

Now work forward and backward in rows, beginning the first row by switching the work to the left hand without turning and pulling the yarn around behind the work, as in the basic I-cord.

Row 1: Knit.

Row 2: Purl.

Row 3: K1, m1, k1tbl, m1, k1 (5 sts).

Row 4 and all even rows: K1, purl to last st, k1.

Row 5: K2, m1, k1tbl, m1, k2 (7 sts).

Row 7: K3, m1, k1tbl, m1, k3 (9 sts).

Row 9: K4, m1, k1tbl, m1, k4 (11 sts).

Row 11: K5, m1, k1tbl, m1, k5 (13 sts).

Row 13: K5, sl2, k1tbl, p2sso (11 sts).

Row 15: K4, sl2, k1tbl, p2sso (9 sts).

Row 17: K3, sl2, k1tbl, p2sso (7 sts).

Row 19: K2, sl2, k1tbl, p2sso (5 sts).

Row 21: K1, sl2, k1tbl, p2sso (3 sts).

Row 22: Sl1, p2tog, psso (1 st). Fasten off.

Make 9 leaves in various shades of green.

Finishing

Attach 7 leaves to the crown of the hat, leaving a space in the center for the rabbit. Sew the rabbit securely in place. Weave in any loose ends. Sew the remaining 2 leaves just under the brown and orange garter stitch border, to the right of the rabbit.

Plum in the Garden

I made this hat after an afternoon of gardening with my little cat Plum. There is nothing he loves more than poking around in the pots, often digging out the little seedlings I have planted and knocking over the containers. Make your playful kitten in the color of your choice.

Size

To fit 18 months to 2 years

Materials

1 x 50 g ball brown DK yarn
1 x 50 g ball terracotta DK yarn
1 x 50 g ball yellow-green DK yarn
1 x 50 g ball orange DK yarn
1 x 25 g ball gray lace-weight mohair yarn
1 x 25 g ball other gray lace-weight yarn (non-mohair)

Small amounts of DK yarn in yellow, sage green, and oatmeal
Small amounts of baby yarn in yellow, orange, cream, terracotta, jade, and sapphire
Size 6 (4 mm) double-pointed knitting needles
Size 1 (2.25 mm) double-pointed knitting kneedles

Size C-2 (2.75 mm) crochet hook
Polyester fiberfill
Cardboard scraps
Yarn needle
Stranded embroidery floss in pink, green, and dark gray
Embroidery needle

Special Stitches

Kt (knitted twirl): With contrasting color and spare double-pointed knitting needle knit into next st and cast on 12 sts. Turn. Bind off.

Mb (make bobble): (K1, p1, k1, p1, k1) in next st; turn, purl next 5 sts; turn, knit next 5 sts; turn, purl next 5 sts; turn. Sl1 knitwise, k2tog twice, psso.

Hat

Using size 6 double-pointed knitting needles and brown, cast on 90 sts. Join to work in round, being careful not to twist the sts.

Rounds 1–10: Knit.

Break off brown and join terracotta DK yarn.

Round 11: Knit.

Join yellow-green.

Rounds 12–25: *K1 with terracotta, p1 with yellow-green; rep from * to end.

Break off yellow-green.

Round 26: With terracotta, purl. Join orange.

Round 27: With orange, knit.

Round 28: With orange, purl.

Rounds 29–30: Knit.

Round 31 (bobble round): K2 with terracotta, *mb with orange, k4 with terracotta; rep from * to last 2 sts, k2. Break off orange.

Rounds 32–33: Knit.

Break off terracotta. Join orange.

Round 34: Knit.

Round 35: Purl.

Break off orange. Join terracotta.

Round 36: Knit.

Round 37: Purl.

Break off terracotta. Join orange.

Round 38: Knit.

Round 39 (knitted twirl round): K4 with orange, *kt with contrasting color, k8 with orange; rep from * until 4 sts from end, k4 with orange. Alternate the colors of the knitted twirls (recommended sequence: green, yellow, oatmeal, green, yellow, green, oatmeal, yellow, green, oatmeal).

Rounds 40–41: With orange, knit.

Round 42: Purl.

Break off orange. Join terracotta.

Round 43: Knit.

Round 44: Purl.

Break off terracotta. Join brown.

Rounds 45–46: Knit.

Join oatmeal.

Round 47 (bobble round): K2 with brown, *mb with oatmeal, k4 with brown; rep from * to last 2 sts, k2. Break off oatmeal.

Rounds 48–49: Knit.

Round 50: Purl.

Join yellow-green. (Do not break off brown.)

Crown Shaping

Work in alternating rounds of brown and yellow-green.

Round 51: *K7, k2tog; rep from * to end of round (80 sts).

Round 52: Knit.

Round 53: *K6, k2tog; rep from * to end of round (70 sts).

Round 54: Knit.

Round 55: *K5, k2tog; rep from * to end of round (60 sts).

Continue decreasing in this pattern until 10 sts remain.

Break off yarn, thread through rem sts, pull up tightly, and fasten off. Weave in all ends on wrong side.

Leaves

With size 2 double-pointed needles and DK yarn, cast on 3 sts. Work an I-cord as follows: *Knit all sts. *Do not turn.* Switch right-hand needle to left hand and pull sts to other end of needle. Pull yarn firmly around behind work, ready to knit into the first st again. Repeat from * until I-cord stem measures 1 in.

Now work forward and backward in rows, beginning the first row by switching the work to the left hand without turning and pulling the yarn around behind the work, as in the basic I-cord.

Row 1: Knit.
Row 2 and all even rows: Purl.
Row 3: K1, yo, k1, yo, k1 (5 sts).
Row 5: K2, yo, k1, yo, k2 (7 sts).
Row 7: K3, yo, k1, yo, k3 (9 sts).
Row 9: K4, yo, k1, yo, k4 (11 sts).
Row 11: K5, m1, sl1, m1, k5 (13 sts).

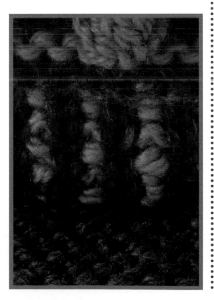

Rows 13 and 15: Knit.
Row 17: K1, ssk, k7, k2tog, k1 (11 sts).
Row 19: K1, ssk, k5, k2tog, k1 (9 sts).
Row 21: K1, ssk, k3, k2tog, k1 (7 sts).
Row 23: K1, ssk, k1, k2tog, k1 (5 sts).
Row 25: Ssk, k1, k2tog (3 sts).
Row 26: Sl1, k2tog, psso (1 st). Fasten off.

Make 4 in sage green and 4 in yellow-green.

Flowers

With size C-2 crochet hook and baby yarn, ch 4. Join with a sl st to form a ring.
Round 1: Ch 2, 9 sc in ring, join with sl st in beginning ch-2. Fasten off.
Round 2: Join contrasting yarn. Ch 3, dc in each of next 9 sc, sl st in last ch of beginning ch-3. Fasten off.
Make 12 in assorted colors.

Finishing

Weave in ends and form into a neat round shape.

Flowerpots

Using size 1 knitting needles and terracotta baby yarn, cast on 30 sts.
Row 1: Knit.
Row 2: Knit.
Row 3: Purl.
Rows 4–9: Rep rows 2–3.
Row 10: *K3, k2tog; rep from * to end of row.
Row 11: Purl.
Row 12: Knit.
Row 13: Purl.
Row 14–15: Knit.

Row 16: *P2, p2tog; rep from * to end of row.
Row 17: Knit.
Row 18: *P1, p2tog; rep from * to end of row.
Row 19: K2tog to end.
Break off yarn, thread through rem sts, pull up tightly, and fasten off. Make 3.

To Make Up With right sides together, sew side seam. Weave in ends and insert a piece of cardboard cut to the size of a coin into base of pot. Stuff firmly with polyester fiberfill to make a rounded shape. Sew three flowers to the top of each flowerpot, sewing the edges of the flowers to each other and to the edges of the flowerpot so that the stuffing is completely covered. There will be 3 flowers left over.

Kitten

Head

Using size 1 knitting needles and 1 strand of lace-weight mohair yarn and 1 strand of other gray lace weight yarn held together, cast on 8 sts.
Row 1: Purl.
Row 2: Kfb across (16 sts).
Row 3: Purl.
Row 4: K2, kfb in next 2 sts, k11, kfb in next 2 sts, k3 (24 sts).
Row 5: Purl.
Row 6: K3, kfb in next 2 sts, k13, kfb in next 2 sts, k4 (28 sts).
Row 7: Purl.

Row 8: Knit.
Row 9: Purl.
Row 10: Purl.
Row 11: K4, k2tog twice, k13, k2tog twice, k3 (24 sts).
Row 12: Purl.
Row 13: K3, k2tog twice, k11, k2tog twice, k2 (20 sts).
Row 14: Purl.
Row 15: K2, k2tog twice, k19, k2tog twice, k1 (16 sts).
Row 13: P2tog to end.
Break off yarn, thread through rem sts, pull up tightly, and fasten off. Sew side seam, leaving a gap for stuffing at the back of the head. Gather the cast-on stitches and fasten off. Stuff firmly. Sew up gap.

Face

Using 3 strands of green embroidery floss, work a couple of straight stitches for the eyes, and then a bullion knot on each side of the center point.

Using 3 strands of pink embroidery floss, stitch a pink triangle for the nose and a few straight stitches for the mouth.

Form the whiskers from single strands of dark grey embroidery floss. Be sure to knot them firmly so they can't be easily pulled out. Tie off all the embroidery floss under the neck, where it will be hidden where the head attaches to the body.

Legs and Body

Using size 1 knitting needles and 1 strand of lace-weight mohair yarn and 1 strand of other gray lace-weight yarn held together, cast on 6 sts.
Row 1: Kfb across (12 sts).
Row 2: Purl.
Row 3: Knit.
Row 4: Purl.
Rows 5–12: Repeat rows 3–4.
Break off yarn and leave live sts on needle.
With new yarn, repeat rows 1–12 for second leg.
Row 13: Holding first leg and second leg with right sides together, knit sts together (knit first st from leg 1 together with first st from leg 2 and repeat across, binding legs together).

Row 14: Purl.
Rows 15–28: Repeat rows 3–4.
Row 29: *K2, k2tog; rep from * to end (18 sts).
Row 30: Purl.
Row 31: *K1, k2tog; rep from * to end (12 sts).
Row 32: Purl.
Row 33: K2tog across.
Break off yarn, thread through rem sts, pull up tightly, and fasten off.

Finishing

Sew leg seams with reverse stockinette side (right side) out. Stuff paws firmly, then close tummy seam, leaving a gap for stuffing the body. Stuff firmly. Attach head above paws, angling slightly to give the kitten a cheeky look.

Ears

Using size 1 knitting needles and 1 strand of lace-weight mohair yarn and 1 strand of other gray lace-weight yarn held together, cast on 7 sts.

Rows 1–4: Knit.
Row 5: K2tog, k3, k2tog (5 sts).
Row 6: K2tog, k1, k2tog (3 sts).
Row 7: Sl1, k2tog, psso. Fasten off. Make 2.

Sew the ears securely on each side of the head.

Tail

Using size 1 knitting needles and 1 strand of lace-weight mohair yarn and 1 strand of other gray lace-weight yarn held together, cast on 2 sts.

Row 1: Kfb, k1.
Row 2: Kfb, p2.

Row 3: Kfb, k3.
Row 4: Kfb, p4.
Row 5: Kfb, k5.
Row 6: Kfb, p6 (8 sts).
Row 7: Knit.
Row 8: Purl.
Rows 9–12: Rep rows 7–8.
Row 13: K6, k2tog (7 sts).
Row 14: Purl.
Row 15: Knit.
Row 16: Purl.
Rows 17 and 18: Rep rows 15–16.
Row 19: K5, k2tog (6 sts).
Rows 20–24: Rep rows 14–18.
Row 25: K2tog across. (3 sts)

Break off yarn, thread through rem sts, pull up tightly, and fasten off. Fold tail piece in half widthwise and sew side seam. Sew onto the kitten so that the tail sits up jauntily. Knot a length of yarn around the kitten's neck for the collar.

Finishing

Weave in all ends neatly. Securely sew the kitten to the center of the crown. Sew the three flowerpots around the kitten. Sew the three remaining flowers to the top of the hat, in front of the kitten. Finally, sew the eight leaves evenly around the edge of the crown.

Rabbit on a Hat

Who could resist this dear little rabbit sitting among the flowers on the top of this cosy beanie? If the hat is for a boy, you could omit the flowers.

Size
To fit 2–4 years

Materials

1 x 50 g ball white DK yarn
1 x 50 g ball aqua DK yarn
1 x 50 g ball bright blue DK yarn
1 x 50 g ball medium blue DK yarn
1 x 50 g ball white baby yarn
1 x 50 g ball blue baby yarn

Small amounts of baby yarn in bright blue, yellow, white, and medium blue
Black stranded embroidery floss
Pink stranded embroidery floss
Size 5 (3.75 mm) double-pointed knitting needles

Size 1 (2.25 mm) double-pointed knitting needles
Size C-2 (2.75 mm) crochet hook
Yarn needle
Polyester fiberfill

Hat

Using size 5 double-pointed knitting needles and medium blue DK yarn, cast on 92 sts.

Rounds 1–10: Knit.
Break off medium blue and join bright blue and white DK yarn.
Rounds 11–22: *K2 bright blue, p2 white; rep from * to end.
Break off white.
Round 23: Knit.
Round 24: Purl.
Break off blue and join white.
Round 25: Knit.
Round 26: Purl.
Break off white, join aqua.
Round 27: *P3, (k1, yo, k1) into same st; rep from * to end.
Rounds 28–29: *P3, k3; rep from * to end.

Round 30: *P3, k3tog; rep from * to end.
Rounds 31–32: Purl.
Round 33: *P1, (k1, yo, k1) into same st, p2; rep from * to end.
Rounds 34–35: K2, *p3, k3; rep from * to last 4 sts, p3, k1.
Round 36: Slip last k1 of of previous round from right needle to left needle, and mark as new beginning of round (this st will be knit again in this round). *K3tog, p3; rep from * to end of round.
Rounds 37–38: Purl.
Rounds 39–44: Repeat rounds 27–32.
Break off aqua and join white.
Round 45: Knit.
Round 46: Purl.
Join bright blue.

Rounds 47–48: With bright blue, repeat rounds 45–46.
Rounds 49–50: With white, knit.
Rounds 51–52: With blue, knit.
Rounds 53–54: With white, knit.
Round 55: With blue, knit.
Round 56: With blue, purl.
Break off bright blue and continue in white.
Round 57: Knit.
Round 58: Purl.
Break off white. Join medium blue.
Round 59: Knit.
Round 60: Knit, decreasing 2 sts evenly.

Crown Shaping

Round 61: *K7, k2tog; rep from * to end (80 sts).
Round 62 and even rounds: Knit.
Round 63: *K6, k2tog; rep from * to end (70 sts).
Round 65: *K5, k2tog; rep from * to end (60 sts).
Continue in this pattern until 20 sts remain. Break off yarn. Thread through rem sts, pull up tightly, and fasten off.

Rabbit

Head

Using size 1 double-pointed knitting needles and white baby yarn, cast on 9 sts. Join to work in round, being careful not to twist the sts.

Round 1: Knit.

Round 2: *K1, m1, k1, m1, k1; rep from * to end of round (15 sts).

Round 3: Knit.

Round 4: *K1, m1, k3, m1, k1; rep from * to end (21 sts).

Rounds 5–7: Knit.

Round 8: *K1, k2tog, k1, k2tog, k1; rep from * to end (15 sts).

Rounds 9–10: Knit.

Round 11: *Ssk, k1, k2tog; rep from * to end (9 sts).

Round 12: Knit.

With sts still on needles, stuff head with fiberfill.

Round 13: *K1, k2tog; rep from * to end (6 sts).

Break off yarn and thread through rem sts; pull up tightly and fasten off. Run a gathering thread around opening at other end of head and close securely. Set head aside.

Ears

Using size 1 knitting needles and white baby yarn, cast on 3 sts.

Row 1: Purl.

Row 2: Kfb, k1, kfb (5 sts).

Row 3: Purl.

Row 4: Knit.

Row 5: Purl.

Rows 6–15: Rep rows 4–5.

Row 16: Ssk, k1, k2tog (3 sts).

Row 17: Purl.

Row 18: Sl1, k2tog, psso. Fasten off. Make 2.

Body

Work the body in alternating stripes of 2 rows white and 2 rows blue. Using size 1 double-pointed knitting needles and white baby yarn, cast on 9 sts. Join to work in round, being careful not to twist the stitches.

Rounds 1–4: Work rounds 1–4 of head.

Round 5: Knit.

Round 6: *K1, m1, k5, m1, k1; rep from * to end (27 sts).

Rounds 7–13: Knit.

Round 14: *Ssk, k5, k2tog; rep from * to end (21 sts).

Round 15: Knit.

Round 16: *Ssk, k3, k2tog; rep from * to end (15 sts).

Round 17: Knit.

Round 18: *Ssk, k1, k2tog; rep from * to end (9 sts).

Stuff the body with fiberfill. Break off yarn, thread through rem sts, pull up tightly, and fasten off. Run a gathering thread around hole at other end and secure firmly.

rabbit on a hat **151**

Arms and Legs

Using size 1 double-pointed knitting needles and white baby yarn, cast on 2 sts. Make an I-cord as follows: *Knit all sts. *Do not turn.* Switch right-hand needle to left hand and pull sts to other end of needle. Pull yarn firmly around behind work, ready to knit into the first st again. Rep from * until I-cord measures 2 in. K2tog. Fasten off. Make 4.

Feet

Using size 1 knitting needles and blue baby yarn, cast on 3 sts.

Row 1: Purl.

Row 2: Kfb, k1, kfb.

Row 3: Kfb, p3, kfb.

Row 4: Knit.

Row 5: Purl.

Row 6: Knit.

Rows 7–8: Rep rows 5–6.

Row 9 (ridge row): Knit.

Row 10: Knit.

Row 11: Purl.

Row 12–13: Rep rows 10–11.

Row 15: Ssk, k3, k2tog.

Row 17: P2tog, p1, p2tog tbl (3 sts). Bind off.

Make 2.

Fold the foot in half at the ridge line and sew edges together. Sew feet to legs with narrowest part of foot facing forward.

Paws

Using size 1 knitting needles and blue baby yarn, cast on 1 st. Make bobble as follows: (K1, p1, k1, p1, k1) in same st, making 5 sts from one; turn. P5, turn. K5, turn. P5, turn. Sl1 knitwise, k2tog twice, psso. Fasten off. Run a gathering thread around the outside and form into a small ball.

Make 2.

Sew to the ends of the arms.

Tail

Make as for the paws but using white yarn.

Scarf

Using size 1 double-pointed knitting needles and blue, cast on 3 sts. Work in garter st until the scarf is long enough to knot around the rabbit's neck. Add a short fringe on each end using a yarn needle or a crochet hook.

Finishing

Sew the head to the top of the body with the nose pointing forwards. Sew the ears in place, making a small pleat at the bottom to help them stand up. Center the tail on the back, a little higher than the legs, and attach the arms to the shoulders. Knot the scarf around the neck. Sew the legs to each side of the body so the rabbit can sit down. Using black embroidery floss, embroider the eyes, using straight stitches or French knots. Sew a nose with pink embroidery floss.

Flowers

Using size C-2 crochet hook and baby yarn, ch 6. Sl st in first ch to form a ring.
Round 1: Ch 1, work 11 sc in ring, sl st into beginning ch-1. Fasten off.
Round 2: Join contrasting color in sl st of prev rnd. (Ch 11, sl st in next st) 12 times; sl st in same st as joining. Fasten off neatly. Make 7 in different shades of blue, yellow, and white.

Finishing

Sew one flower to the center of the crown and then sew the rabbit securely on top. Sew the remaining flowers around the top of the crown.

Daisy Mouse

This cute beanie is knitted as a tube and gathered at the top like a paper bag. Peeping out from the top is a cute little mouse. If you leave off the flowers, this would be a lovely hat for a boy.

Sizes
To fit 12–18 months (2–3 years)

Materials

1 x 50 g ball cream DK yarn

1 x 50 g ball French blue DK yarn

Small amounts baby yarn in navy, light blue, white, and fawn

Size 6 (4 mm) double-pointed knitting needles

Size C-2 (2.75 mm) crochet hook

Size 1 (2.25 mm) double-pointed knitting needles

Polyester fiberfill

Stranded embroidery floss in pink and black

About 30 in. of $3/8$ in. blue velvet ribbon

Yarn needle

Embroidery needle

Special Instructions

Wyib: with yarn in back

Hat

Using size 6 double-pointed knitting needles and cream, cast on 92 (98) sts.

Join to work in round, being careful not to twist sts.

Work 16 (20) rounds of k2, p2 rib.

Join French blue and knit 1 round.

Begin sl st pattern section:

Round 1: With blue, *k1, sl1 wyib; rep from * to end.

Round 2: With cream, *sl1 wyib, k1; rep from * to end.

Rep rounds 1–2 until work measures 6 (6½) in. from beginning, ending with a row 2.

Break off cream.

Next 2 rounds: *K1, p1; rep from * to end.

Eyelet round: K1, *yo, k2tog; rep from * to last st, k1.

Work another 10 (12) rounds of k1, p1 rib. Bind off in ribbing.

Mouse

Head

Using fawn baby yarn and size 1 double-pointed knitting needles, cast on 9 sts. Join to work in round.

Round 1: Knit.

Round 2: *K1, m1, k1, m1, k1; rep from * to end (15 sts).

Round 3: Knit.

Round 4: *K1, m1, k3, m1, k1; rep from * to end (21 sts).

Rounds 5–8: Knit.

Round 9: *K1, k2tog, k1, k2tog, k1; rep from * to end (15 sts).

Rounds 10–11: Knit.

Round 12: *Ssk, k1, k2tog; rep from * to end (9 sts).

Round 13: Knit.

Leaving sts on needle, stuff head. Break off yarn, thread through rem sts, pull up tightly, and fasten off.

Body
Using white baby yarn and size 1 double-pointed knitting needles, cast on 9 sts. Join to work in round.
Round 1: Knit.
Round 2: *K1, m1, k1, m1, k1; rep from * to end (15 sts).
Round 3: Knit.
Round 4: *K1, m1, k3, m1, k1; rep from * to end (21 sts).
Round 5: Knit.
Round 6: *K1, m1, k5, m1, k1; rep from * to end (27 sts).
Rounds 7–15: Knit.
Round 16: *Ssk, k5, k2tog; rep from * to end (21 sts).
Round 17: Knit.
Round 18: *Ssk, k3, k2tog; rep from * to end (15 sts).
Round 19: Knit.
Round 20: *Ssk, k1, k2tog; rep from * to end (9 sts).

Round 21: Knit.
Leaving sts on needle, stuff body firmly. Break off yarn, thread through rem sts, pull up tightly, and fasten off.

Ears
Using size 1 knitting needles, cast on 2 sts.
Row 1: Purl.
Row 2: K1, m1, k1.
Row 3: Purl.
Row 4: Kfb, k1, kfb.
Row 5: Purl.
Row 6: Knit.
Row 7: P2tog, p1, p2tog.
Row 8: Knit.
Bind off.
Using 3 strands of pink embroidery floss and satin stitch, embroider the inner surface of the ear.
Make 2.

Pinch lower edges together and pin ears to head. Sew securely in place.

Legs, Arms, and Tail
Using size 1 double-pointed knitting needles and fawn baby yarn, cast on 3 sts.
Make an I-cord as follows: *Knit all sts. *Do not turn.* Switch right-hand needle to left hand and pull sts to other end of needle. Pull yarn firmly around behind work, ready to knit into the first st again. Rep from * until I-cord is desired length. Sl1, k2tog, psso, and fasten off.
Make two I-cords 1½ in. long for the arms, two I-cords 2 in. long for the legs, and one I-cord 2¼ in. long for the tail.

Feet and Paws
Using size 1 knitting needles and fawn baby yarn, cast on 1 st. Make bobble as follows: (K1, p1, k1, p1, k1) in same st, making 5 sts from one; turn. P5, turn. K5, turn. P5, turn. Sl1 knitwise, k2tog twice, psso.
Make 4.
Attach one to the end of each arm and leg.

Finishing
Sew the head to the body with the pointy nose at the front and the narrowest part of the body at the top. Using 3 strands of black embroidery floss, make a French knot on each side of the head for the eyes and fasten off where the head joins the body.

Finishing

Thread the velvet ribbon through the eyelet holes. Draw up tightly and tie in a bow. You will now have a little nest for the mouse to sit in. Place the mouse in the nest, facing the same way as the bow, and sew securely in place. Sew five flowers around the top ribbing section, evenly spaced. Sew the last two flowers to the front and back of the hat.

Using the pink embroidery floss, make a French knot for the nose. Sew arms, legs, and tail in place.

Flowers

Make 7 in various color combinations.

With size C-2 crochet hook and baby yarn, ch 4. Join with a sl st to form a ring.

Round 1: Ch 2, 9 sc in ring, join with sl st in beginning ch-2. Fasten off.

Round 2: Join contrasting yarn. Ch 3, dc in each of next 9 sc, sl st in last ch of beginning ch-3. Fasten off.

Weave in ends and form into a neat round shape.

Embroidery Stitches

Many of the hats included here are decorated with embroidery stitches as well as knitted ornaments. Before embroidering on the hat, try out each stitch first on a spare piece of fabric to make sure you are happy with the yarn as well as the embroidery.

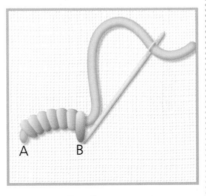

Backstitch

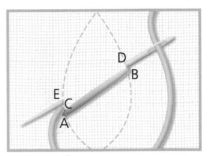

Satin stitch

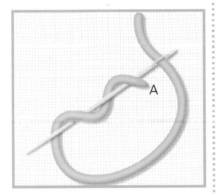

French knot stage 1

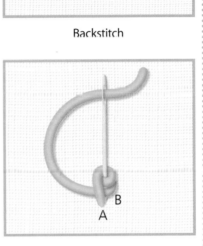

French knot stage 2

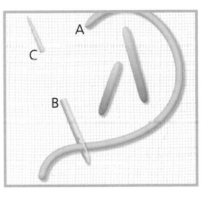

Straight stitch

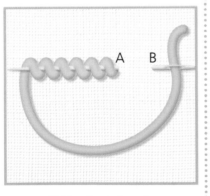

Bullion knot stage 1

Bullion knot stage 2

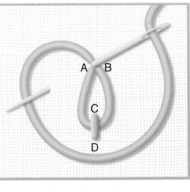

Lazy daisy stitch